INSIDE A POLICE INFORMANT'S MIND

INSIDE A POLICE INFORMANT'S MIND

Paul Derry

CRC Press
Taylor & Francis Group
Boca Raton London New York

CRC Press is an imprint of the
Taylor & Francis Group, an **informa** business

CRC Press
Taylor & Francis Group
6000 Broken Sound Parkway NW, Suite 300
Boca Raton, FL 33487-2742

Printed on acid-free paper
Version Date: 20150623

International Standard Book Number-13: 978-1-4987-1535-5 (Hardback)

Visit the Taylor & Francis Web site at
http://www.taylorandfrancis.com

and the CRC Press Web site at
http://www.crcpress.com

MIX
Paper from
responsible sources
FSC   FSC® C013056
www.fsc.org

Printed and bound in Great Britain by
TJ International Ltd, Padstow, Cornwall

Encouragement from any source is like a drop of rain upon a parched desert. Thanks to all the many others who rained on me when I needed it, and even when I foolishly thought I didn't.

—Claire Gillian

There have been a select number of people who have especially been my encouragers, and I dedicate this book to them:

- *To my family, who surround me with love on a daily basis. Your patience has been outstanding, overwhelming, and deeply appreciated.*
- *To those in the crime world, on both sides of the line, who still communicate with me and help to keep me safe while being hunted.*
- *To my best friend since childhood, Garth Wooster, who, up until days before he died last year, continued to give me a hard time for using his first name as an alias for 30 years.*
- *To my father, Brian Derry, who passed away before ever getting to see the drastic changes for the better that took place in my life.*
- *To my ex-wife, who will never know how often she has been an inspiration to me rather than a hindrance. Unfortunately, we made better partners in crime than we ever did partners in marriage.*
- *To Sean Simmons and his family. Unfortunately, there is nothing I can say that will make things better.*
- *Last of all, to every first responder, every ambulance driver, firefighter and police officer, down to the last person to leave the scene of any required call. You are overworked, underpaid, and not nearly as recognized as you ought to be for the hell on earth that you witness each and every day.*

Paul Derry

Contents

Section I
MOTIVATIONS OF AN INFORMANT

Section II

CHARACTERISTICS OF A
STRONG SOURCE HANDLER

Contents

Acknowledgments

A storyteller makes up things to help other people; a liar makes up things to help himself.

—**Daniel Wallace**
The Kings and Queens of Roam

Where does one begin to thank and recognize all those who have helped to make something like this possible? I guess I should start at the beginning. Inevitably, that means that I should begin with RCMP Deputy Commissioner Mike Cabana. Had it not been for him, I would not be here today (although I admit that assertion can be taken several different ways). It has been an honor and a privilege to work with a person who has demonstrated so much balance and integrity over all of the years that I have known him. It is even more of an honor to consider him my friend. (Mike, I don't have many friends, so would you please fake it for the sake of the book?)

Deputy Commissioner Mike Cabana

I consider Mike a friend, and I also consider the other main character in this book a close and personal friend. There have been very few people who have believed in me as much as Shane Halliday. When you take into consideration that he is the homicide detective who arrested me, our relationship becomes even more baffling. For whatever reason, Shane and his wife Aileen have believed in me for the past 15 years, even when they were ridiculed for doing so. I want to thank them and publicly promise them that, although I am still a work in progress, their belief has not been in vain.

Shane Halliday rookie photo from 1972

While I am thanking friends, I cannot forget my best friend and fiancé Kris, a woman with the heart of a servant and the patience of Job. This book would not have happened without her.

I hate to admit it, but my closest friend after Kris is a lawyer. Darryl Lucke has been my lawyer and my friend for many years. If there is someone who breaks the stereotype of a lawyer, he is the one. Throughout our friendship, he has protected me even when it incurred the disapproval of his peers, he has represented me when I needed advice, and he has, in humility, come to my defense as a friend time and time again.

I am thankful to the following friends:

- Bruce, a mentor and Christian leader, who told me how to write a book: "Start at the beginning and write." That may seem like simple advice, but that is exactly what I did.
- Dean, a great friend and teacher, who did more research and document reading than any lawyer would ever dream of doing.
- Alice, a wonderful woman (and a great lawyer) who has poked, prodded, encouraged, and helped tremendously throughout the entire process of writing this book.

I also thank Wallis Zbitnew, a Rotarian, who gave me a copy of her book, *Mr. Apple Discovers the Four Way Test.* This book helped me to see a way to make fair decisions in all aspects of my life.

My thanks also go to several other people who worked with me to make this book happen:

- Confidant Communications, for their work on the graphics of both of my books.
- Crime reporter Gary Dimmock. It was he who planted the seed that I should write a manual for police to use when dealing with informants.
- Development editor James R. Coggins. I could never have finished this book without his constant pushing and encouragement.
- Darryl Plecas, a great criminologist, who convinced me that I had knowledge that others could benefit from.

I offer special thanks to Taylor & Francis Group and CRC Press and all of their staff for taking this book on as a project.

Last of all, I want to thank all of the police officers who spent hour after hour in both conversation and debate with me. Similarly, I offer my thanks to prosecutor Peter Craig and his staff for all they endured in their dealings with me from day one.

Introduction: The Making of an Informant

All human beings, as we meet them, are commingled out of good and evil...
I saw that, of the two natures that contended in the field of my consciousness,
even if I could rightly be said to be either, it was only because I was radically
both.

—**Robert Louis Stevenson**
The Strange Case of Dr. Jekyll and Mr. Hyde

The strong wind mixed with ocean spray coming off the Atlantic onto the beach at Lawrencetown, Nova Scotia, made me shiver. Or maybe it was the clothes covered with brain matter and blood that we were trying to throw into the open sea. Everything seemed surreal. Less than an hour before, we had been having a beer and chilling out, and now we were destroying evidence after helping to take a man's life.

I tried to keep focused as we buried the gun and threw away the evidence, but it was difficult. I remember stopping for a minute on a bluff overlooking the beach. As I watched my girlfriend, down on the water's edge, throw item after item as far out as she could, memories began to flood my mind. I could not help but wonder how I had managed to become such a monster.

The flashbacks came to me so clearly. Thirty years earlier and not three hundred yards from where I was standing, my family had picnicked on that same beach. I could see in memory my dad throwing us around in the water. Meanwhile, my mom was putting out the blankets and opening up the Tupperware containers of peanut butter and jam sandwiches that were just a little too warm from the sun. Sand in the picnic lunch, ice cold water that gave us a brain freeze, playing catch along the beach, hiding in the sand dunes—who would have thought that one day I would bring to that place of summer innocence the horrors of a murder?

From the innocence of childhood to the reality of a Hells Angels–ordered killing—what twisted journey would take a person from one to the other? When did the innocence stop and the evil begin? How did a young boy full of love and life change into a lying, thieving killer who hated almost everyone he met? That is a difficult question, but I will do my best to answer it by sharing some of the thoughts I dredged up as I searched through my own fragmented mind.

Role-Playing Practice

Since this book is about the world of informants, police agents, and their handlers, I should start at a place that may shed some light on the root of my narcissism and my fascination with the shadowy world of undercover operators. I will go back to where my journey began, long before the insanity became the norm for me.

It was back on that beach on the Atlantic Ocean that my imagination began to run wild. If you can picture or remember a time when there was no Internet, no video games other than those at the arcade, and not much entertainment other than that which we created from our own minds, then you will probably understand that role playing was a key ingredient in our fun and excitement in childhood. It did not matter if we were playing cowboys and Indians with our air rifles, pretending to be characters from our favorite TV shows or playing my favorite game, cops and robbers, it was all about roles and the acting. The beach at Lawrencetown was a place where I and my brothers, without all of our friends, had the opportunity to practice many of these games. Although it was just the three of us—with sometimes a little help from a real soldier, our dad—this was where I perfected my role-playing abilities.

Back home, on the military base in Greenwood, Nova Scotia, I continued to indulge in these imaginative games. Day after day, I joined a group of friends riding around the base on our bicycles playing cops and robbers as if we were the real deal. The group always included my friends Gunner Grolman and Daryl Perry. Gunner went on to be an awesome musician, Daryl became an RCMP officer, and, ironically, I became a criminal. Why is that ironic? Because my initials were PD—which stood for Police Department in our little minds—I usually played the cop, and Daryl usually played the robber. I hated the role but played it anyway.

The games I played as a boy are important because being an informant is all about playing a role, playing many roles. I believe that the imagination I employed and the seriousness with which we played helped shape my ability to immerse myself in roles. They also show that I seem to have decided early on that I wanted to be a robber and not a cop.

I should probably point out that I am a bit of an extremist. Even at that age, I took everything to its limit. When Gunner went home after we had played cops and robbers, he would do his homework, maybe play some guitar or plan for some upcoming role in a drama club production. When Daryl went home, he would do similar things—do homework, prepare for football, or pursue his hobbies. Not me. I went to bookstores and libraries to find any book on criminals I could get my hands on—*The Outsiders, Go Boy, Bingo, The Last Mafioso*. By the end of grade six, I was reading books on the police and criminals—no longer for play but now to understand how to live out these roles.

I know it seems strange, crazy, weird, or even insane, but that's the way my brain worked. That is when the first seeds were planted in my mind. As I cultivated them, they grew. Eventually they blossomed, to the point that a seasoned witness protection coordinator would say, "Derry is the most manipulative bastard I ever met." It was somewhere back then that I began to lose myself in the roles I was playing. Somewhere back then, playing roles for fun changed into living out roles for gain, and the little boy grew into a monster. It was back then that the first of two distinct personalities was born.

Dr. Jekyll and Mr. Hyde

I need to delve a little deeper into this, as I believe it is the only way that you will understand how I dealt with the chaos of my journey. What were these two distinct personalities? Simply, I saw myself as both a Dr. Jekyll and a Mr. Hyde, a good guy and a bad guy. I don't mean a "Robin Hood" kind of good guy. I was not out to rob from the rich to give to the poor, although I did. I was not a bad guy trying to appease a guilty conscience by doing good, although I did. I really did see myself as two different characters in one body. There was Paul Derry the good guy, the honorable man who hated criminals. Then there was Paul Derry the bad guy, who was dedicated to the criminal lifestyle with all of its glamor; this Paul Derry did not have any honor and did not care who got hurt in the process.

Imagine for a moment that you could do anything you wanted. Imagine you could steal money, have all the sex you wanted, hurt anyone you hated or anyone who just pissed you off. Imagine you could give in to all of your desires. What would that look like? What was life like for Paul Derry the career criminal?

Pretend for a minute that you are a voyeur looking into my house in Brockville, Ontario, catching a glimpse of my lifestyle through my window from across the street. Better yet, imagine you are a cop doing surveillance on me back in the day. Here is a typical picture of what you might see:

Couches, loveseats, and chairs line the walls almost in a complete square around the perimeter of the room, a room filled with some of the most dangerous people you could ever meet. There are two bikers from Montreal, the driver for a Mafia boss in southern Ontario, a man who is affectionately known as the "Freak" and who lives up to his nickname, an ex-con who has just been released from prison after serving a sentence for murder and a former member of the Canadian Armed Forces Airborne Unit, which has been disbanded. In the center of the room are two naked women performing at the commands of those watching; nothing is taboo, and not one order is ignored or refused. In the kitchen, which is just around the corner from this den of entertainment, are pounds of cocaine and ounces of speed being divided up for street distribution, with the crumbs going to the entertainers and guests in the other room. Just off the kitchen and outside the back door is a van filled with an arsenal of guns, ammunition, and explosive devices, waiting to be used in a drug war or to be offered for trade on the drug market. In the bedroom is Tina, my girlfriend and partner, who is home after a week of stripping in a club in Ottawa; she sits on the bed with a guitar in her hands singing Janis Joplin tunes as she lets the drug of the day flow through her veins.

That is quite a picture from the outside looking in, but that was probably pretty "par for the course" for my life in those days. That is how Paul Derry the career criminal lived.

Now imagine that you could do all this and there would be no consequences. Imagine you could steal money, have all the sex you wanted, hurt anyone you hated, give in to all of your desires and not suffer any consequence from your conscience or society. What do you think you would need to do to be able to live that "take what I want" lifestyle? How did I get to live that life of a bad guy? How did I protect my lifestyle that allowed drugs, sex, and crime to flourish?

For that, you will have to look at the other personality of Paul Derry: the good guy, the honorable man who hated violent criminals. It was the good guy who protected the bad guy and allowed him to survive. The police informant was dependent on the criminal for the information he sold, but the criminal was dependent on the informant for his existence. It was the informant who allowed the criminal to survive.

My previous book *Treacherous* describes my role in a Hells Angels contract killing. In the end, I entered Canada's Witness Protection Program and received a new identity. In the process, I eventually killed off both versions of Paul Derry and have become someone quite different. I received a pardon after 12 years of giving back to society. Now I am hoping this book will help others understand a little more about the crazy world I used to live in and the roles I used to play.

Author

Paul Derry walking along the Atlantic coastline

Paul Derry was first used as a source for the Royal Canadian Mounted Police (RCMP) when he was under the age of 18. He was coded officially in 1988 and worked as a source until the year 2000. His career ended October 3, 2000, after an attempted operation went horribly wrong, resulting in the death of Sean Simmons. After the Halifax Regional Police Department arrested him for the murder, he agreed to provide information on the other participants in the murder in exchange for immunity from prosecution. As a consequence, Derry and the members of his immediate family were placed on a Hells Angels hit list, and in May 2001 they were placed in the Witness Protection Program in order to ensure their survival.

Since leaving the world of crime behind, Derry has made some drastic changes in his life:

- He has received a federal pardon from the Canadian government.
- He has served as a director for a nonprofit organization that works with victims of violent crime.
- He has worked as a consultant regarding many areas of the criminal justice system.
- He has worked in Christian ministry, with a focus on preventing youth from entering gangs and helping those involved in gang life to escape its grasp.
- He authored the book *Treacherous: How the RCMP Allowed a Hells Angel to Kill*.

- He participated in a documentary based on his book, done by E1 Entertainment and aired as part of the series *Outlaw Bikers* on the History Channel and the National Geographic channel.
- More about Paul Derry can be found on the website www.paulderry.ca. He can be contacted at info@paulderry.ca

Motivations of an Informant

I

1

Motivations of an Informant

Blood Brothers

1

Hell is the highest reward that the devil can offer you for being his servant.

—Billy Graham

It would be awesome if all crimes were solved instantaneously the way they are on TV shows like *CSI*, *Criminal Minds*, or even *The Sopranos*. It would be great if all crimes were quickly figured out by DNA or other technology. But this is not reality. Although these forensic tools often help prove guilt and sometimes point out targets, the majority of suspects are found out by the use of human sources.

What does the term "human source" mean? In the criminal world, a human source is referred to as a stool pigeon, a snitch, or a rat—unless the snitch is an undercover cop, in which case he is referred to as a narc.

Since this book is going to focus mainly on one type of human source, the confidential informant, I thought it best to give a few definitions that are not so derogatory. Keep in mind that these are my definitions, based on how I perceive the law to define them.

1. *Source:* Any person who gives information to the police. A source is often someone who is not involved in the criminal subculture.
2. *Confidential informant:* Any person who gives information to the police and who requests and receives assurance of confidentiality.
3. *Police agent:* An informant who takes the next step and is being directed by the police to gather information.
4. *Handler:* A police officer who is designated to deal with an informant or agent. This is usually an officer who has taken the initiative to form a relationship with someone in the criminal world and build up some trust.

The relationship between the human source and the handler is the crux of this book. It could be compared to a marriage—but it would be an abusive, controlling, manipulative, deceitful, and dysfunctional one. What makes it all the more interesting is that both sides enter into the relationship knowing this and yet go on to trust each other with their lives.

This is probably a good place to point out that from a police organization's perspective, this marriage can be a troublesome arrangement. This is illustrated well by an assessment from my former handler and now RCMP deputy commissioner, Mike Cabana: "Human sources have always been considered an organizational resource. Unfortunately, over the years, many investigators who manage sources have considered them personal resources. While they have a responsibility to their source, the organization needs to ensure an appropriate level of governance is maintained over this handler/source relationship. This is as much for the benefit of the organization as it is for the benefit of the source and handler."

The Agent's Perspective

As a confidential informant, I have had to deal with my share of police officers through the years. Many of these officers considered themselves my handlers. However, from my perspective, I have only ever had one person I fully believed to be my handler. This person was so trusted by me that I would refuse to work as an agent, pass on information or even work in another jurisdiction without his approval. Is this unusual? I don't think so, but I am only able to respond from my own perspective. In my mind, it would almost have seemed adulterous to flirt with the idea of using someone else without talking to Mike. Once I was committed to him, it was for better or worse, in sickness or in health, until death would part us. There is a myth that informants are not loyal. From my perspective, it was not that I was not loyal, but that I chose who would get my loyalty and nobody else mattered.

So, what was I looking for in a permanent handler? There was and is no shortage of cops handing out business cards. There was no shortage of officers stopping their cruisers to make a quick joke or try to engage me in small talk. They used one gimmick or another to try to build rapport. How did I filter through them all and finally pick Mike?

I would like to say that it was because I knew that one day Mike Cabana would become an RCMP deputy commissioner. It would be a hell of an ego boost to insinuate that my discernment was so keen. However, that is obviously not the case. I will note that the qualities of character he displayed as a constable are the same ones that have carried him up through the ranks to his present position.

In the beginning, it might have been the nice red Audi sports car that Mike was driving, along with the fact that he was in amazing shape. I know that sounds as if I am joking, but truly I am not. There was a lot more to these two aspects for me.

First, the sports car was Mike's personal car, and he drove it quite often, on his own time, to the Tim Horton's where we tended to congregate as street-level drug dealers. It was during these quick stops, seemingly to grab a coffee, that he would tell a joke or say something witty. It showed him as just a guy, not an authority figure.

Second, Mike worked out daily at the Gold's Gym a couple of blocks from this same Tim Horton's. Many times, I would see his car or see him coming or going in his workout gear. Day and night, it seemed he lived police work and had an addictive hobby of working out.

Why did these things impact me as much as they did as a potential informant? Partly because of the contrast with some of the other recruiters, the more typical ones. They, too, would swing by the Tim Horton's, usually during their shift and in their patrol car. They would make a smart ass remark to try to sound tough or look cool, and then usually try to give us a card as they drove away. Their approach struck me as egotistical. I am not saying all other cops did this, but that was the norm, and cops like Mike were the exception. I got the feeling that for some the doughnuts were the priority rather than cultivating an informant. I did get to see many of the doughnut eaters when they were off duty, usually at one of the bars that we knew cops liked to go to for a beer after work on Fridays. It was always great fun to see how much we could provoke them when they were out of uniform.

First impressions are everything in building a relationship of any kind, but especially one which will require you to risk your life. I wanted the in-shape, muscular cop who ate, slept, and breathed his job. I did not want the cop who ate, slept, and lived in his cruiser and then partied to escape the horrors of his difficult career. This is not to say that all of those cops at the bar were there to party, any more than all of us were there to provoke them, but many of them, and us, were there for just those reasons.

The Handler's Perspective

I am not even going to try to answer why Mike picked me to cultivate as an informant. I am, however, going to try to answer a question that gets asked by people all the time: Why do police make deals with the devil?

Brian N. Cox, a former RCMP and NCIS officer and author of *How to Solve a Case: Criminal Investigation for Police Officers*, explained:

"The average young uniform police officer may or may not be a detective/investigator in the future as he gains more experience. Nevertheless, whether he is a detective or a uniform officer, one of the best ways he can combat crime is to recruit confidential informants. The confidential informant is the 'eyes and ears' of the police officer within the criminal underworld. Without these informants, police officers will have little chance of learning what is happening within their own territory. Techniques to recruit confidential informants should be taught in basic police training so that each officer leaves the training college with the ability and the goal to develop his own informant network. It is a fact that of all the cases the police are called upon to solve, that involve offences committed by professional criminals or criminal gangs, confidential informants are utilized in the majority of cases that are brought to a successful conclusion. The importance and value of confidential informants in police investigations cannot be overemphasized."

A good friend and former homicide detective, Shane Halliday, summed it up more succinctly: "If all we ever use are altar boys, all we will ever catch are priests."

Shane Halliday working undercover during Operation Download

The criminal world is a world where there is no value on human life, a world where you can be killed for something as simple as taking a piece of cheese without asking or calling someone a goof. It is a world in which you should tread lightly. If you are going to walk into that world as a police officer, then you had better learn quickly that you are the most valuable trophy for those in that world who hunt humans. A police source is usually right next in line behind police officers as a target. So, why would anyone want to "sleep with the enemy"? What in the world would make anyone in either one of these two groups want to jump into bed with someone in the other and make the risk of dying even higher?

I do not believe that most police officers want to risk their lives any more than they have to in a day, but some understand better than others what is necessary to do their jobs well. There are those who barely build a network of informants and usually solve crimes by chance or through their colleagues' sources. Then there are those who build enough of a network of informants to get their job done each day and get home. Last, there are those who build a network of informants that is exceptional because of its quality and quantity. These are the ones who will benefit the most from this book.

Why do cops make deals with the devil? Actually, they make deals with the demons in hopes of taking down the devil. That is why they jump into marriage with the enemy. But, before they do, it is best if they get to know the demon they are dealing with.

Blood Money

2

Nothing is easier than to denounce the evildoer; nothing is more difficult than to understand him.

—**Fyodor Dostoyevsky**

The punching bag swung back, hitting against my chest after I threw the last and hardest punch. I could barely lift my arms and was almost dropping from exhaustion as the last of my breath escaped my aching lungs. The sweat poured from my head, and my eyes stung from the intense workout. I looked up in time to see Sylvan stepping out of his Cadillac and heading toward me. I was happy to see him but a little nervous about the huge man who seemed to be shadowing him like a bodyguard. It was good that Sylvan had driven the six hours to see me; that likely meant he had the cocaine that I was wanting to front from him. It was not so great that he wanted to emphasize what would happen if I did not pay him the money for the drugs. This was clearly why he had brought along the steroid king with the nine millimeter in his waistband.

Sylvan was heavily connected to the Hells Angels in Montreal through a puppet gang and really did not need to demonstrate his power; with or without the bodyguard, I was quite aware that not paying for two kilos of cocaine would mean a bad ending for me. I guess knowing that the steroid king would enjoy causing me pain made Sylvan feel a little more secure in the transaction.

To give an idea of what was at stake, let me explain the finances involved in the transaction. "Fronting" means that I would be given the drugs on credit. The cost of one kilogram of cocaine on a front at that time was $52,000. If the money was paid at the point of purchase, then it was around $45,000–$48,000. The terms would usually be fifteen days per kilo fronted.

Seven years earlier, another well-connected drug dealer had stopped by my house to bring me some fresh lobster. It was in a small fishing village near the Quebec/New Brunswick border, and I had gone there specifically to scope out the town's drug dealers. This dealer fronted me two kilos of hash when dropping off the treats from the sea. The cost of one kilogram of hash on a front was around $7,000 at that time.

What neither of these men knew is that in both cases I was also working with the police, in the first case as an informant and in the second case as an agent. Why would I do this? The most common motivation police usually write down in their source assessment reports is financial gain. Let's take a look at what I was paid by the police.

Police Pay

As an agent for the police in a mid-level drug operation back in the 1980s, I would receive the following amounts:

- Housing—$750 per month
- Utilities—$200 per month
- Vehicle (rental)—$800 per month
- Allowance—$2,000 per month

That adds up to a monthly total of $3,750. A typical operation of this nature could last for three to six months, with an additional payout of anywhere from $2,000 to $10,000 per target upon arrest. Since most of the targets would be mid-level dealers, $2,000 would be the norm and $10,000 would be the rare exception. So, altogether, in a six-month operation with ten targets, I would receive $20,000 in cash plus $22,500 for living expenses, for a total of $42,500. That amounts to a little over a couple of hundred dollars a day but more than half of it in expenses.

I am sure that sounds like pretty good money, especially when the minimum wage was around five dollars an hour. However, considering the risks that were involved and the amount of hours worked, it wasn't that good.

But it was still a lot better than the amount given to informants. At least, as an agent, I was signing a contract at the beginning, a price was negotiated ahead of signing, and therefore the payment was guaranteed upon delivery of each target. In contrast, as a coded informant, I would gather the information and then try to negotiate a price based on the value of the information I was providing. The bottom line is that for every hundred dollars I perceived the information to be worth, I was lucky if the powers that be saw it as worth twenty dollars. It was a negotiation in which the police had all the power, and they did not like letting go of cash. As an informant in the first case, if I was a decent negotiator and was in a jurisdiction with money, I could set up Sylvan and get paid a couple of thousand dollars.

Looking at these two cases, was it worth the money? Was there enough cash involved to motivate me to live with the risk of being killed? An agent can sometimes hit the jackpot, but those are rare operations. The direct amount paid to an informant may seem good on the surface, but I could make the same amount selling pot at a low level with very little risk. Lots of people would see this direct pay as a good living, especially drug addicts whose addictions won't let them see past their next fix. But a low-level drug user will only be able to provide information on low-level drug dealers, not the ones at the top.

The Real Money

From a monetary perspective, the real motivation for someone like me was not what came to me directly as an informant or agent but what came indirectly. Let's go back and look at the same two examples I used before, starting with Sylvan.

Sylvan's certainty of being paid for those two kilos of cocaine was only a delusion. Sylvan's bodyguard could flex his muscles all day long and act as tough as he wanted, but it wouldn't make any difference. The reality of what would likely happen is this. Sylvan would come back in two weeks to a month and get paid for the drugs he had left behind. We would probably celebrate over a dinner and a scotch, or maybe we would enjoy an evening like the one I described earlier that a watcher might have glimpsed through my window. Regardless, Sylvan and his goon would expect me to need more drugs each time they came to visit me. At some point, they would be comfortable enough with me to bring a sizable amount of cocaine.

Let's assume I owed them for three kilos and they were traveling with at least as much. I would make a call, they would get busted in a routine traffic stop, and they would be off to jail for the next two to three years. I might get a couple of thousand dollars from the police, but the real benefit would be that I would be up 3000 grams of cocaine. When mixed with "cut," it would be closer to 5000 grams, making it worth anywhere from a quarter to half a million dollars on the street.

In the second example, the operation might be a little more controlled and therefore require a little more finesse, but I could use the same basic plan. If I knew the date the operation was going to end, I would borrow as much money as I could and front as much dope as I could before that end date. That is why it was important to me, whether acting as an informant or as an agent, to gain as much control, or at least as much information, regarding the takedown date, as possible.

The point I am making is that of course an informant is motivated by money. And many informants are motivated by the small direct amounts that will pay for a few days of escape from reality, whatever that escape may be. However, for those who have been around long enough to learn how to play the game, there are many more ways to make money indirectly and many more reasons for informing in general. For example, when a man like Sylvan goes down, it offers an informant like me the opportunity to acquire more customers and the ability to climb the ladder a little more.

Something else important needs to be said. Besides the monetary motivation, there are deeper reasons for becoming an informant. There is a saying that pimps have been using for a long time when trying to recruit a new girl to prostitute for them. It is used in a derogatory way toward women. However, I have always thought it a perfect fit regarding informants—"You all get paid; just some take cash."

Streets of Blood

3

Don't believe everything you hear:
Real eyes, Realize, Real lies.

—**Tupac Shakur**

Traffic creeps slowly through the city, carrying home the many in society who have just finished the nine-to-five shift. They have poured their blood, sweat, and tears into another day and are looking to reenergize their weary bodies and minds. The majority are returning to homes that they hope are comfortable, safe, and secure sanctuaries. They hope to raise their families in a moral environment that allows them to live in harmony with the rest of the community. Most are probably walking into their homes thinking about not much more than what is for supper or whatever event they, their children, or their spouses have planned for that evening. I don't assume every law-abiding citizen is experiencing this, but, based on the thousands of *normal* families I have gotten to look at over the years, this attitude seems to be more the rule than the exception.

In contrast to this prosocial world, there is another world that is very antisocial, the somewhat disorganized yet organized crime world. This is a world at war with all that would stop it from existing. Everyone knows it is there, but most try to keep it hidden in their TV sets or behind the wall of police officers who are paid to keep it away. Unfortunately, it does coexist, hiding within the normal world and often colliding with it—even when the police are doing all that they can to not let that happen.

The Criminal World

During this same time period, when most in society are coming home from a hard day's work, most criminals are preparing for their work. The drug bosses are dropping off supplies of drugs to secure locations across the city. Their soldiers are taking these drugs to fortresses to be portioned for distribution on the night shift, flooding the streets with drugs of every kind. There will still be enough drugs left over to supply a skeleton crew for the day shift.

Meanwhile, groups of thieves and units armed for home invasions are plotting out the areas that they will attack as they get their tools together. Many of these people are strung out and needing to feed their demons.

The spotters are preparing to follow police officers, suspected informants, and anyone who may be a danger to this culture, its income, or its leaders.

The enforcement teams are going out to collect debts owed from any number of criminal schemes and ventures—from drugs and prostitution to extortion of business owners.

The elite soldiers of the night are the crazed hit men. They are tasked with hunting down and killing whoever may be on the list they have been given that week, and sometimes some additional names they have been given at a moment's notice. The presence of these killers is widely felt, but they are rarely seen. If you do see them, it's usually because you are one of them or your time is up.

There is one thing of which you can be certain. These criminal outfits— thieves, pimps, drug dealers, and killers—are strategizing mayhem each and every night. They are going out knowing it could be their last night of freedom, their last night in that particular trade, or possibly even their last night on earth. Some go out with a sense of desperation, which makes them unpredictably dangerous, but all go out with the knowledge that there is a criminal hierarchy, a criminal organization. They might not know who all the players are, but they know they are a part of this organization. Although most criminal leaders sleep through the night and try to blend in with society during the day, they are in control at all times—even when they are in prison.

This is a glimpse into a world that runs twenty-four hours a day, seven days a week. It is an industry, a huge money machine, which runs on blood, sweat, and tears and in which people are dispensable. It is a world at war, which produces casualties on an hourly basis. Take a peek inside an emergency room on any given night, and you will see the broken, stabbed, shot, and drugged bodies of the casualties. The ambulances drop them off, and the police write up their reports quickly and head back out for more, waiting for the next call to bring in a perpetrator or a victim.

The World I Lived In

This is the work environment I lived in as an informant and a criminal. It is the place that I felt driven to stay in, a place I thrived in. It is a puzzle of a world in which I not only got to see the pieces, but got to move and manipulate some of those pieces as well. By being in the unique position of playing both sides, I had the ability to change parts of the picture.

I have stated earlier that money was a motivator, but not in the way that is usually thought. I wanted to be paid, of course. But there is no way you could ever convince me to sneak around among cons and killers, break bread with them and their families, and then have them sent to jail for the amount of money a police officer makes—and certainly not for the few dollars offered to me as an informant. My monetary gain came, for the most part, from my ability to manipulate people, including the police.

What did it take for me to sneak among cons and killers in order to bring them down? In order for me to go into a den of vipers, I had to become a snake who would fit into that den, all the while knowing that I would be protected as an informant. Being an informant was a workplace safety mechanism. It allowed me to be an evil criminal no different from any of those I would take down—but with some extra tools to manipulate the system.

A Short Sentence

In 1991, I was in the Moncton Detention Centre, doing eleven months for a number of counts of fraud and theft. It was only a month or so before my second child would be born and weeks away from Christmas. I was desperate to get out in order to be there for the birth of my son and to be able to look after my five-year-old daughter while my girlfriend was in delivery. My desperation was growing by the day, and my calls to Mike Cabana were becoming dangerous, as I was risking exposing myself as a rat.

On an eleven-month sentence, it is nearly impossible to receive any kind of parole, as an application takes an average of six months to process. This did not deter me at all, and my calls and letters not only continued but increased. As I became more despondent, I looked up every loophole there was in the system and passed it on to Mike. I reminded him of the many favors that I had done for him, including the information I had provided to him for next to nothing in pay, and I promised to provide more in the future.

Mike made no promises other than that he would look into what he could do within the parameters of the law and without doing anything that would reflect negatively on the justice system as a whole. In the end, he was able to have me released to a halfway house with strict conditions that allowed me to finish my sentence in the community and be there to help my girlfriend during the birth of my son.

Mike Cabana during a press conference on organized crime

On the surface, this seems like a logical favor that probably could have been done by a case management officer without any influence from a police handler. However, as Paul Harvey used to say, "Here is the rest of the story":

I had started this eleven-month sentence not long after I had done a police operation in northern New Brunswick in which I had helped to take down a number of high-profile targets. When I entered the correctional center, I was suspected of being a police informant, and I was double-bunked with a high-ranking member of the city's largest and most dangerous crime family. This not only made for some sleepless nights, but it required a lot of storytelling and explaining. I was fortunate that this guy was giving me the benefit of the doubt, but even he was having a difficult time sticking up for me. The family had already taken out a contract to have me killed, and although he was doing everything possible to negotiate on my behalf, it was not looking good.

I was literally sick to my stomach. But Jim-Bob finally gave up and changed ranges, essentially cutting off all negotiations and leaving me vulnerable, at the mercy of the rest of the prisoners. That was why I made the decision to push Mike to get me out of there under any pretense possible. At the same time, I asked him to put me in touch with another member of the police force, with the promise that I would undertake another operation if they got me out of there. I thought this might improve Mike's bargaining power on my behalf.

The baby being due soon, the promise of another operation and Mike's concern for my safety all helped to secure the favor I needed. That favor set a precedent. For the next twenty years, requesting favors was one more vital tool I used to protect myself as both a criminal and an informant, a tool that offered workplace safety. Although favors are expected—it is a give and take business—like most informants, I pushed to get every advantage I could. These favors increased my leverage as a criminal and benefited more than my handler.

This story not only shows how favors were expected and given, but it also touches on another one of the motivations for working as an informant.

Dealing with Fear

Obviously, I experienced a fair amount of fear as prisoners started to turn against me during that eleven-month sentence. This was not the only time that I called on Mike to get me transferred due to danger and not the only time that I used the RCMP in general to protect me.

Shortly after escaping the grips of Jim-Bob, I was at home and enjoying Christmas with my newborn son when I noticed a suspicious car scoping out my house from across the street. After a few minutes, I realized that the car contained two hit men who had been sent to kill me. I watched for hours in the hope of getting out of the house and away from my family. After twenty-three hours, I finally caught a break as they drove to the store to get something to eat. My bags were packed, and I decided to make a run for it. I kissed my family goodbye and ran for my '71 Camaro parked about three blocks down the street.

As I jumped into the car and started the engine, I saw in my rear-view mirror the two killers speeding down the street toward me. I slammed the car into drive and peeled away. I knew that it would be impossible to lose them. There were no cell phones back then, and stopping at a payphone was out of the question—they would have just shot me in the phone booth and left me there as a deterrent to other informants.

I had run out of options, and my adrenaline was pumping. I decided to go where I knew I could find safety—the nearest RCMP detachment. I was hoping that Mike was working that day, but at that point I really did not care. I pulled up to the building, yet it did not seem to be deterring the killers in the least. I thought they were going to shoot me right outside the detachment. I reached the doorway just as an officer was leaving the building. He listened to my story and then headed toward the two well-known gangsters. After yelling a few derogatory remarks, they said that they would see me again and that I could not run forever.

I spent the next five hours at the police station while the other officers got in touch with Mike and decided what their next move should be. It was decided that they would escort me back to my house to get a few more belongings and then to the highway, so I could leave town for a while. I was never so happy to be on the open road and heading for Ontario, yet I was devastated that I had had to leave my family behind—all over a lousy $5000 contract on my life.

This was one of the many times when Mike, the RCMP, or other police forces did me favors or protected me from my criminal enemies. Sometimes they were protecting me from my own paranoia, and sometimes, as in the case just mentioned, they were protecting me from real and valid threats.

Ulterior Motives

Not all the times that I turned to my handler for protection were for reasons related to my work as an informant. The reality is that most of the time my reasons were much more manipulative, such as using the police to protect my criminal empire. It is almost impossible to climb the ladder in the criminal world without making enemies. Those enemies will usually try to take you out in order to take your position or territory. Although climbing that ladder helped me provide the police with bigger and bigger targets, the truth is that I was sometimes doing it more to advance my career as a criminal than for more honorable reasons.

In 1996, I was dealing with the Halifax Hells Angels and was moving up the ladder quickly as I helped to control strippers and the cocaine supply in that area. In the process of moving up in that world, I was putting many small and mid-level dealers out of business. This was obviously good for me both as a criminal and as an informant; however, it was also making me many enemies. On top of that, I was also getting in over my head with my drug debts. My first priority was to keep alive. In order to do that, I needed to start taking out some of my enemies before they decided to take me out. As I did not want to kill these people in a literal sense, I did what I knew best. I composed a list of targets that the police would be happy to take off the streets while also eliminating all of my enemies.

Although this particular operation did not work out—it was cut short when I went back to prison—it shows that there is almost always an ulterior motive for an informant's actions.

Paranoia and Diversion

The last thing I would like to touch on in this area is the paranoia I experienced and one way which I dealt with it.

For an informant, paranoia can come from either side of the crime world. It can come from criminals who you think are out to get you, or it can come from police officers who don't know you are an informant. There is a saying that "Just because you are paranoid, it doesn't mean they are not out to get you." I had a witness protection handler tell me recently that it must be a scary way to live thinking that the police are always out to get you. In hindsight, I suppose she was right. However, I do not believe I would have been as effective as an informant if I had not always lived by that assumption.

I found the best way to deal with the issue of paranoia was the easy way, the same way I used to get rid of competition—divert the heat to others.

I once called Mike and asked if I was under investigation for drug dealing, as I was getting stressed by seeing marked police cars go by my house every day. Mike's response was simple and has stuck with me all of these years: "If you can see them, you probably have nothing to worry about." Even though that helped me with my paranoia, I still found it easier to keep the police busy by feeding them other fish.

To sum up, the criminal world is a work environment that very few choose to go into, one marked by violence, bigotry, and greed. It is one that even cops hesitate to go into without uniforms, guns, and cover teams. It is a world informants must blend into in order to gather information, in hopes of selling it and receiving all the benefits possible. For the most part, informants operate without any type of morals and definitely without any rules—something the police are unable to do.

The Thrill and Excitement

4

I know that if I wasn't scared, something's wrong, because the thrill is what's scary.

—**Richard Pryor**

There are many motives for becoming a police informant or working as an agent. One that was pretty high on my list of reasons was the sheer excitement of it all. It is not necessarily something I recognized back when I was involved in the work, but it is certainly undeniable in hindsight.

A Day's Work

Early on a weekday morning, three of us sat in a car across the street from a tobacco factory. The day would probably have seemed long and boring to others. For hours, we sat and watched as one tractor-trailer after another backed up to the dock to be loaded with its expensive cargo. We stared as box after box, each containing fifty cartons of smokes, was packed into the trailers until they could hold no more. As each truck drove away, we would copy down the number that identified the trailer the tractor was hauling.

That part of the job may have been mundane, but by nightfall the excitement and thrill would be overwhelming.

As the working day for most people came to an end, ours would just be beginning. The first thing we would do is go to a local dealer and rent a U-Haul truck, using one of the fake sets of identification we kept for just such an occasion. Then we would drive the truck to the industrial park and park it in one of the larger lots. That way, it would be easily accessible yet not quickly noticed by any nosy employee. With all now in place, we would wait for dark.

The excitement, derived from fear, would begin as we drove our car to the highway which ran alongside the industrial park. The excitement would grow as we left our car on foot, armed with handguns, flashlights, and the list of numbered trailers that we hoped to locate. The plan would usually be for two of us to find cover and watch for the patrolling security guards, who would make their rounds every fifteen minutes to a half hour. The third person would scour the area looking for one of our intended targets. Sometimes it would take minutes, sometimes it would take hours, but we rarely left empty handed.

When a trailer was found, one of us would go to get the U-Haul, one would keep watch, and the third would use bolt cutters to snap the lock on the back of the trailer. In five minutes, we could usually throw at least twenty to thirty boxes into the U-Haul and be on our way. At a thousand dollars a box on the black market, that was a pretty good score for a day's work.

The money was great. But the excitement was something else. It's hard to put into words the feeling we got while creeping through a maze of buildings and tractor-trailers knowing that at any minute we could be busted or, worse, shot. Our hearts would be pounding in our chests while we rushed to accomplish all that we had to do in a brief, fifteen-minute period, all the while wanting to turn and run. It was more than exhilarating.

The only thing that could make it just a little more exciting, just a wee bit more nerve-wracking, is that through the entire process I was gathering information and working my way from the bottom of the criminal organization to the top. I was looking to find out who sold the guns that were used, where the smokes went when they were sold, and who was trading drugs for the smokes. Above all, I was hoping to find the mastermind who had all the power, who had planned the operation, and who had sent these soldiers out to do the work. It took a number of these nights and many moments of panic before all was done and those around me were all arrested. It was the ultimate thrill for me, better than sex but with the same pattern of foreplay, a climax, and then a time of rest. Who could ask for more from a job?

Adrenaline Rush

Charles Caleb Colton wrote, "To know the pains of power, we must go to those who have it; to know its pleasures, we must go to those who are seeking it: The pains of power are real, its pleasures imaginary."

For me, the thrill of the crime was real, the excitement of the bust was beyond comprehension, and the mixture of the two was an addictive drug that I still crave today.

Only an hour before I sat down to write this chapter, I was on my way home from the grocery store and once again found out just how strong my attachment to the thrill of policing still is. As I was about to pull out into traffic, an undercover police car, with no sirens going but with lights flashing, soared by me at a high rate of speed. Seconds later, another car, this one marked, flew by, going even faster, again with the lights flashing but no siren.

I literally had to force myself to pull over and stop myself from following. What's worse is that even though I chose not to follow, I sat there for the next ten minutes reminiscing with my girlfriend about all the takedowns that had involved cars racing to the scene just like the ones I had just seen and how I had often been right in the middle of it all. I could feel the thrill again in every bone in my body.

I often wonder if that sense of excitement will ever go away. If I am being truthful, I really hope it doesn't. I believe that it indicates I have a true empathy for those who risk their lives daily to keep society safe. However, there is something that I believe even more strongly: It is that the thrill of the hunt, the thrill of the bust, and the thrill of the takedown give such an adrenaline rush that it is hard to walk away from the life that offers them. I know I will never find anything that can possibly replace that rush.

Cold Call

In the meantime, there are other ways to gain an approximation of the thrill that I can never regain. The Hells Angels have had a contract on my life for the past fourteen years. Not long ago, I ended up standing behind a full patch Hells Angels member at the checkout counter at Walmart. As we stood in line, I struck up a conversation with him, and I ended up leaving the store with him. By coincidence, his vehicle was parked beside mine. By the time we stopped talking and were parting ways, I had his phone number and an agreement to meet the next day to buy some hash from him.

Now, of course, I did not meet him. In fact, I got into my car and then called my Witness Protection coordinator to pass the information on to him. It was exciting to know I can still do a cold call.

I could write chapters filled with incidents just like this one. These incidents have helped to amuse me now that I can no longer work in the criminal world. But it is highly unlikely that my skills will ever be put to work for real again.

Cold Blooded

5

I don't care what you think unless it is about me.

—Kurt Cobain

They say there is a fine line between a police officer and a criminal. They both live every day in the same cold-hearted world of death and destruction, among all the sins of society. In the case of the police officer, there is a line that does not get crossed because the police officer has a moral compass and compassion for others. In the case of most career criminals, there is also a line that does not usually get crossed, but this is due to fear and an instinct for survival.

An informant is different. He lives in both worlds, crossing that line as needed—sometimes for survival but more often to feed his own narcissism. In my case, I got off on the fact that I could travel back and forth between the criminal world and the normal world using information as a tool. Information allowed me to remain in control and feed my self-centeredness.

Breaking Bread with My Target

Wayne and I sat at the kitchen table, laughing as we told jokes, razzed each other over past exploits, and made plans for future deals. As we sipped a cold beer and reminisced, we expressed our appreciation and admiration for each other at least six or eight times. As we sat there, my girlfriend served up a hot pork roast. Breaking bread with my partner and longtime close friend was enjoyable but not altogether innocent. After finishing our meal, we headed out to the balcony, where we could discuss certain criminal business more privately—at least, Wayne thought it was private. I was secretly recording our conversation on the balcony as we discussed a murder that had been committed and other murders that were being planned. When I had recorded enough information to incriminate Wayne, we went back in to enjoy a few more beers and watch a movie. Ironically, the movie was *Donnie Brasco*, the story of an undercover cop who lived covertly for six years among the Mafia.

After the movie, Wayne and I walked down to his car, with me still wearing the wire and trying to get every last bit of information out of him before he left to go home. We gave each other our normal hug and handshake, and Wayne drove off. As I walked back up the stairs to my apartment, I thought about what Wayne was about to go through. I thought about how he would pull up to his house in Uniake Square and the sinking feeling he would have as the police cars blocked him in and officers with guns drawn took him into custody. I thought about his long ride to jail, where he would likely spend the next twenty-five years.

Then I opened the door to my apartment, erased it all from my mind, grabbed a piece of meat off the plate on the table and headed to a safe house to hand over the tapes to the police.

Revenge

Cold blooded? Yes, it was cold, but that was the norm for me. I was able to turn my conscience off and on without any trouble at all, like a light switch switching from light to dark and back again. I was self-centered, focused on myself and myself alone.

The next time I saw Wayne was in a courtroom as I testified against him in his murder trial. As I looked into his eyes, I knew what he was thinking; he believed that this was revenge for something he had done years ago. It was not true, but I could see in his dark eyes that he thought this was the reason for my betrayal.

But that does not mean that revenge was never a motive. I often said, "Vengeance is mine, saith Paul." If I didn't like something another criminal had done, I would make a call and get him or her busted. I did not play the revenge card often, but it was among the motivations I have used at least once.

Although Wayne James was one of those I ratted on for revenge, it was not when I testified against him regarding the Hells Angels hit he was on trial for. That had occurred years earlier.

Back in the early 1990s, while I was doing a sentence in the correctional center, Wayne had gone to my house and slept with the mother of my first child. In the circles we both traveled in at that time, that act would normally have gotten him killed. However, since Wayne was married to my cousin, I really did not see having him killed as an option. He was also a hit man and someone very difficult and expensive to take out.

I decided that I would just keep it to myself and do what I did best. I waited and studied, I listened and gathered information—and when I had enough information, I made the call. Wayne was picked up on suspicion of dealing drugs while on parole and for traveling outside his jurisdiction without a travel permit from his parole officer.

If I am being honest, there was a sense of satisfaction in being able to bring Wayne down the second time, but this was only slightly because he had wronged me. The truth was that Wayne was a killer, one of the elite I spoke about earlier going out with one purpose: to kill.

Easing Guilt

The good thing about playing god—being an informant—is that it helped me deal with my own guilt. When I did not like something I had done, I would take down a bad guy, and I would feel better. If you would have asked me fifteen years ago, I probably would have told you that this was one of my key reasons for being an informant. Turning in other criminals for doing bad things was almost a form of penance for the bad things I had done myself.

It seemed that most of my life there had been a fight between good and evil going on inside me. The easiest way I had found to deal with this constant battle—which I always seemed to be losing—was to pay off my conscience. Unfortunately for me, guilt is not appeased by cash, drugs, alcohol, or women. I did find out, though, that each of these four things made my guilt somewhat bearable, and doing good deeds almost made my behavior seem acceptable.

I am no Robin Hood who stole from the rich to give to the poor. However, I was a rat who did not mind throwing others under the bus in order to feel better about the wrongs that I had committed myself. In the end, it took a permanent change for the good to finally give me some peace in regard to the guilt and shame I felt because of the life I had once loved and hated.

A Pat on the Back

The police make use of many informants each year and more than their share of agents. But, in my mind, I was the one and only, the top dog. I was convinced that crimes could not be solved without me. Do not get me wrong. I was good at what I did, and without that god complex I would not have been nearly as good. However, my arrogance made for difficult working relationships, putting a strain on everyone involved.

To tell the truth, I did not care. I was looking for kudos. I was looking to have my ego stroked on a constant basis. I was very aware that each time I did something that got the police an arrest or closer to one, I would get a pat on the back. The more pats on the back, the more likely they were to overlook my bad behavior.

My god complex was related to my need for kudos and attention—from the good guys and the bad guys. In this vein, I should explain the notoriety I had in the criminal world. Although I wore many hats in that world, being known as a drug dealer among other things, my real specialty was fraud. There is no surprise there, I am sure. I was always considered a money maker, but my real skill became evident when bank cards first came into existence and I started doing bank card fraud. I became so addicted to it that the criminals said I should have a bank machine in my bedroom for foreplay. Prison officials sent me to a twelve-step program to get help specifically for this issue.

Why is this important? For two reasons. First, as I said, I received praise everywhere I went among the bad guys for my ability to rob banks of hundreds of thousands of dollars. The second reason is the practice it gave me in deception because of its similarities to the role playing of an informant. Without going into a lot of detail, I will show how a typical monthly scam worked.

Taking the Train

Stepping up to the wicket at the train station in Halifax was always exciting for me. With anywhere from three to five Royal Bank cards in my pocket, I could not help but smile as I purchased a Canrailpass. It was an invaluable tool to me as a fraud artist, as it allowed me twelve days of travel, to be used within thirty days, at a cost of a little more than three hundred dollars. I loved trains, I loved playing roles, and I loved money; these trips were literally more exciting to me than sex.

Stepping onto the train, I usually skipped right by my seat and went down to the bar car. I would scope out the car and see the type of clientele before deciding what my name or occupation would be for that trip. I have pretended to be everything from a military diver to a loans manager for the bank that I planned to defraud.

As I said, the train pass allowed for twelve days of travel, to be used within thirty days. Leaving Halifax, I could travel to Vancouver in six days, party for a few days, and then travel back to Halifax in five more days. I would take advantage of the many one-hour and two-hour stops along the way to make deposits and withdrawals using the bank cards and spreading the scam from one end of the country to the other. Not only did this make me a lot of money, but it also allowed me to make many connections along the way.

Building a Career

Being known as a money maker in a world of greed, along with the ability to make connections, was invaluable to my work as an informant. However, as I said in the beginning, being an informant was also invaluable to my work as a fraud artist, helping me to be successful at making money. I was a career rat but also a career criminal; I am not always sure which came first. I do know, though, that to be good at any career, you have to devote your life to the occupation and to studying how to do it better. In prison I studied the criminal world, and on the streets I studied the police as I worked with them.

As revealed before, my motivations for being an informant included

- Money
- Revenge
- Diverting police attention to other criminals
- Getting rid of competitors and advancing my career
- Obtaining protection from criminal hit men and police investigators
- Reducing my fear and paranoia
- Obtaining favors from the police
- Appeasing my conscience
- Narcissism and massaging my ego
- The thrill and excitement

This list does not include all possible motives, but it does show the main reasons most informants do the work. In the next chapter, I am going to outline what I always considered one of my main motivations—and certainly one of the most important ones if I was going to keep my criminal life safe: becoming an informant to study the police.

Police Study

Rouse him, and learn the principle of his activity or inactivity. Force him to reveal himself, so as to find out his vulnerable spots.

—**Sun Tzu**
The Art of War

If there is a curiosity I have in regards to the criminal world and a good majority of those involved in it, it revolves around the haphazard way in which ninety-nine percent of criminals do business. No matter what career you choose in life, there are some common keys to success; those keys also apply to the world of crime and to informants.

Police forces around the country spend twenty-four hours a day, three hundred and sixty-five days a year in the study of criminals. They take courses to continually keep up with changing trends, they gather intel from human and nonhuman resources, they share information, they hold conferences, and they live in community with others who work in similar occupations. Police also contract with profilers, analysts, criminologists, and psychiatrists. Police keep their minds sharp and their bodies in shape. They practice the skills they learned in basic training until they are proficient and those skills become second nature. Last but not least, they have available to them spiritual advisors to help them retain their moral compasses. They practice accountability with each other and outside teams.

In contrast, the criminal world for the most part is made up of dysfunctional and uneducated individuals. They tend to learn from prisoners (those who have failed in their profession by being caught) and from what they see on TV. The police are motivated by a desire to give back to society and a sense of pride and honor. Criminals are motivated by greed and an arrogant and ignorant sense of pride and self-centeredness.

As an informant, self-preservation was usually a very high priority for me. My belief was that if you were going to fight battles or be a part of any type of war, then you should know the enemy. If you were going to take on any career, then you should school yourself in everything to do with that career.

As I said, I had already made up my mind that I wanted to be career criminal at a young age and started studying all the books I could find on criminals and their trade. However, unlike many criminals, who spend their lives in and out of jail, I also wanted to understand my adversary as well as humanly possible. Considering the fact that I weaved in and out of both worlds, adapting like a chameleon to my surroundings, I thought it best to know both sides equally. After all, one mistake in either could cost me my freedom or my life. This was one of my last motivations for being an informant but possibly the most important—and one that police officers should grasp and not take lightly when dealing with informants.

Controlling Conversations

By being an informant, I was able to spend countless hours in conversation with many police officers. This was sometimes on the phone but most often in person. It could be at a detachment, in a back alley, in a motel room, or in a large public parking lot. Wherever it was, the conversation always contained the same elements: they were reading me, and I was reading them. As I often say, conversation is like boxing—in order to throw a punch, you have to open yourself up to taking a punch. In other words, all conversation is give and take; if you give up information, you can gain information as well.

Studies have concluded that sixty to ninety-three percent of our communication is nonverbal. If you ask any police officer or friend who has dealt with me, they will all agree on this: that I hardly ever stop talking. There are two reasons why this is so, and it is both a blessing and a curse. The first reason is that I process information by speaking out loud. I find that I understand my thoughts much better when I hear them out loud and have a sounding board by which to gauge reactions. The other reason is that when working as an informant and gathering information, it is more important to pay attention to the nonverbal communication than to the words that are spoken. I have found over time that most people in the criminal and police worlds lie or exaggerate. On the other hand, nonverbal communication cannot be faked. Therefore, it is best to place very little emphasis on the spoken word but to pay close attention to what is not being said. This is why, when I was in conversation with the police, I would try to keep talking. If I could control the conversation, dictating the subjects, it would give me the ability to gauge the reactions and be able to discern when the police officers were being truthful, when they were equivocating and when they were lying outright.

As a side note, this skill is something that police officers also learn and employ. It is a technique often used in interrogations.

Witness Protection Coordinators

In 2001, along with my family, I entered Canada's Witness Protection Program. There, too, the ability to read each Witness Protection coordinator's nonverbal communication was invaluable. Unlike the RCMP, I did not have the technical resources to analyze every movement, word, or deed. However, I had had the opportunity to observe and learn from many police officers, lawyers, and others who had spent many years reading communications beyond words. In his song "The Gambler," Kenny Rogers commented, "I have made a living out of reading people's faces." That same skill has kept me and many of my kind alive.

It was early in the morning when I stepped into a covert police vehicle for a three-hour drive to prepare for my upcoming relocation. As I entered the car, the silence was deafening. Not a word was spoken for the first hour, other than the mandatory greetings when I got in. This was not something I welcomed but something I had to contend with. The juvenile attitude of animosity displayed by the officer who was in charge of case management and who had a beef with me meant that she had no interest in speaking. It's not that she would not talk, but that she chose only to talk to her partner. For my part, I was content to listen and learn. This officer had had very little time on the force in comparison to most I had met in that unit, and she lacked professionalism, morality and, for the most part, common sense.

I sat quietly for the first while, trying to decide the best way to proceed. It seemed as if the partner she was with was trying his best to make conversation and act as a peacekeeper. I used that to my advantage by engaging in conversation with him while nonchalantly focusing on her. I also sent a text to my girlfriend beside me, telling her to watch the reactions as I directed the conversation. After two hours of nonstop conversation, I was drained. At the end of the day, my girlfriend and I took time to compare notes and discuss what we had observed. We also went over how much information we had given out in order to obtain the knowledge that we had gained.

This is a very mild example, but it shows why controlling conversations is beneficial. In this case, it was strictly to gain information—to understand where we were at in the relocation process, to detect any deceitfulness that might be going on, and to profile those we were dealing with in regards to their strengths, weaknesses, biases, and attitudes. Sometimes, as is the case with many manipulative informants, intelligence gathering can be for much more diabolical reasons.

Gathering Intel for Manipulation

It is not surprising that an informant would collect information. It was a crucial part of our job. Who we gathered information on and what we did with that information would help determine our income and our lifespan. It became an ingrained habit to see all information as something that could be sold or used to our advantage. It was no different in regards to the information we collected on the police. Personally, I would listen and research to build profiles on every officer I dealt with—I catalogued these officers' birthdays, likes, dislikes, addictions, dreams, aspirations, addresses, family information, and anything else that would help me paint a picture of the person I was dealing with.

Why? I wanted to know as much as possible in order to ensure my own safety, to judge whether people were acting with integrity, and to help build relationships in general.

Do all informants collect information as I did? No. Were there times when I used the information I gathered to manipulate other people? Yes. Are there people who use information for even more sinister reasons than I did? Yes.

I can tell you that if they could find a weakness in a police officer, most informants would gladly exploit it. In fact, I would guess that most of us, if we found that officer no longer beneficial to our cause, would use that weakness to destroy that officer. For the most part, I have not deliberately set out to destroy an officer's life. I have tried to manipulate police officers in every meeting I have ever had with them, but my motives were generally mixed with some sense of honor.

The fact remains that I have spent my life digging up dirt on almost every person I could, just in case it might one day give me an advantage. It did not really matter to me if I ever used the information. Often it was enough that the person knew that I had the information available to use.

Thirty years ago, I used to hang around a motel in Moncton, New Brunswick. The owner of the motel was gay, and I spent many nights running over to one of the rooms there to drop off whatever drug his current lover might want. It was not long before I started to meet some of these lovers—a lawyer, a real estate developer, a physiotherapist, and (my favorites) a Moncton city police officer, and a parole officer from the Correctional Service of Canada. Being gay in today's world is not a big issue, but in the early 1980s it still had a stigma attached to it. I bring this up because this was the first time that I realized that building files on people could benefit me in the future. This was proven by the fact that every one of those men did many favors for me without me ever asking for one.

So my practice began. I am certainly not saying I was able to gather dirt on every cop I met. Truly, for some of them, I only gathered enough information to be able to pass on a "Happy birthday," a "Congratulations on another year on the Force" and other, similar pleasantries. But I continued to collect information throughout my career as an informant, especially as I moved up the ladder to outlaw motorcycle gangs.

Information on police was also gathered for much more sinister reasons. Two criminals illustrate this. One was known to police and belonged to a gang. The other may have been known by police but not in any overt way that I can remember. What they both had in common was that they had folders that were filled with pictures, addresses, and other information on the police officers in their area. Both had something else in common—they were violent and they hated cops. Earlier, when I was describing the work environment that I entered each day, I specifically mentioned those whose job it was to follow police and suspected informants. That is precisely what these two individuals were doing. Their first job was to follow suspected police informants and confirm whether they were indeed informants. If they were, that information would be passed on to the hit men. Their other and more important job was to gather all the information they could on every police officer who was working against each cell in the criminal pyramid. The information could include work schedules and shift changes so that the timing for crimes could be perfected. They would also try to get close to officers in the hope of tempting them with money, women, or any other vice to which their surveillance revealed they might be susceptible.

One final thing that has not been discussed previously is that outlaw gangs like to send in "double agents." They will allow their members to become informants in order to learn all they can about police protocols and procedures and to get even closer to investigators for all the reasons already mentioned.

In the early 1980s, I was in jail with a group of guys who had got caught bringing a boatload of drugs into Canada. I became a workout partner with one of them and had many discussions with him about operations like the one in which he had been involved. The one thing that stood out to me was that he said, "One out of three boats gets caught on purpose, to allow the other two to get through." I do not know if that is true, but I do know that outlaw gangs have people rat on a regular basis to help them get away with crimes or to deflect investigations away from themselves. If I had to guess, I would say that my workout partner's statement was true and that the practice he described has most likely increased drastically in the past thirty years.

Pushing Buttons

Earlier, I described my practice of talking constantly in order to direct the conversation and gauge reactions. In fact, often I did not even hear the verbal response and would have to try to remember it later when I was processing what had happened. For the most part, I did not care what most of my conversation partners had to say verbally. I was much more focused on their body language.

For the same reason, I would like to push buttons and try to stimulate an emotional reaction during a conversation, whether it was anger, sadness, or sympathy. It really did not matter which it was as long as I could evoke some kind of an emotional reaction and gain an opportunity to once again read the body language. However, I will also say that when I was pushing someone's buttons, I would listen a little closer to the verbal communication. Why? Just as when they are drunk, when people are emotional, they will say things that they would normally keep in.

To sum up, almost every tool I used to gather information from criminals in order to pass it on to the police, I also used against the police for my own benefit. I could say more but do not want to give away too much in case this is read by the wrong people, who would then use it in an immoral way. Therefore, I will end this section on the motivations and manipulations of informants and move on to the skills and abilities the police must have in order to deal with people like me who are *hard to handle*.

Characteristics of a Strong Source Handler

II

Dedicated to the Job

7

Screams of fright and cries of pain,
The smell of death, a world insane,
Broken bodies, young and old—
Oh, the loved ones who must be told.

Blood and flesh, sirens and lights,
Alleys and bars, hookers and fights,
Sadness, emptiness and despair,
A world of hurt where very few care,

Glass pipes for crack or meth,
Black tar heroin and the needle of death,
Dealing with killers who each carry a gun,
Chasing convicts who are now on the run.

Outnumbered and hated, they start the day.
Where evil reigns, they earn their pay.
Death and destruction is what they see—
Dedicated to the job for you and me.

—Paul Derry

On Friday, May 5, 2006, Constable John Atkinson was shot and killed in Windsor, Ontario, by a man who thought killing a police officer was some sort of badge of honor. "It's the first time in 120 years that a cop was killed in Windsor, and I did it," Nikkolas Brennan was quoted as saying. "I'm getting life for this (expletive). I don't have to worry about paying rent anymore. I better get some respect up in here. I'm a killer…This is the sickest thing I've ever done. It was the highlight of my life, killing a cop." (*The Windsor Star,* October 25, 2007)

The killer was caught and sent to prison for the mandatory life sentence. Unfortunately, one day he will probably be free from his prison. Those who loved Constable Atkinson—his family and friends—will suffer the horrors of that day for the rest of their lives.

Every time I see a police funeral on TV or read a description of one in the papers, I can't help but cry. While I sat and watched the funeral of John Atkinson, I literally sobbed as I listened to the eulogies describing him as a hero, but, more importantly, as a brother, a son, a father, a husband, and a friend. It is what I have seen throughout my career as a police agent—the human side of the uniform. The following letter from a police cadet was among the thousands of condolences expressed for the slain officer. I believe it describes something felt throughout the law enforcement community every time a member falls:

> I am a police cadet. Today, while driving home on a beautiful afternoon after my third day at Ontario Police College, I heard over the radio that a Windsor Police Constable had been killed in the line of duty. Upon hearing the news, the beautiful afternoon I described seemed to have turned dark and gloomy in what felt like an instant, my heart just sank. I felt an overwhelming sense of emptiness and sadness that words cannot describe. The pain felt as if I had lost a sibling. I'm not even a sworn police officer yet, but the camaraderie I have experienced so far with my fellow cadets is so powerful, I cannot imagine how this tragedy must feel for veteran officers. I wish to express my deepest condolences to the family of Constable John Atkinson. I will pray for your untimely loss, and please take to heart the fact that Constable John Atkinson is a hero in life, not in death; his sacrifice will not be forgotten. May we all pay our respects to this fallen officer, whom we are all indebted to for his death in protecting his community.

> **—Mark H.**
> *Richmond Hill, Ontario*

To Serve and To Protect

We all know the part of police officers' job that requires them "to protect." TV often depicts police officers chasing down bad guys and bringing them to justice. As a matter of fact, most of this book revolves around that aspect of policing as well. However, there is much more to policing than chasing bad guys; police officers are also required "to serve." It is in their service that many officers stand out as leaders and heroes. It is their service that we as a society benefit from the most but often recognize the least. It is also in their service that many police officers are pushed to the edge of human ability, pushed beyond what any person should be expected to endure. It is in understanding this dark side of policing that we can truly understand the dedication it takes to do this for a living.

Detective Shane Halliday stated, "Some members of the public think the police only catch bad guys and bother innocent citizens, but they do many things that the public would never think of and many would not want to deal with." It is these many things that the public would never think of and most would not want to deal with that cause police to struggle with a host of issues, including alcoholism, domestic violence, anger issues, and suicide.

When They Break

Because of the evil they face every day, police officers tend to have a very dark sense of humor. Often they have a strangely cynical take on events. Sometimes, despite all of their training, they act in ways that are unbecoming a police officer. It is likely that the outside world, the public, would turn their heads in disgust if they overheard some of the private conversations I have had the opportunity to listen in on. It is easy to be repulsed, disgusted, or even frightened by what police officers might say or do. It is easy to sit back and criticize, like an armchair quarterback after a football game. But, considering what we send cops out to do every day, we should show our respect and appreciation—and not only when one of them is killed. And when a police officer does not act in a way that he or she should, a little empathy is in order before we jump on the media bandwagon and demand an immediate crucifixion. We should not condone actions that are wrong, yet we should let due process take its course.

When They Are Broken

An off-duty RCMP officer pulled onto a lonely stretch of highway in western Canada. It was early, with sunrise about an hour away. The 34-year-old father of two was seen to be driving erratically, and then he turned his car into the path of an oncoming tractor-trailer. Nobody but he and God will know what really happened that morning or what was going through his mind as he pressed the gas pedal and accelerated into the truck. Many in the town think it was a suicide, but if it was, that was never stated publicly.

On average, Canadian police forces lose between 125 and 150 officers to suicide every year. Of course, that number only represents those officers whose death certificates actually say suicide. Unfortunately, suicide among police officers is sometimes looked upon as a weakness rather than as what it is; more often than not, it is a result of trauma experienced over and over until finally the officer simply cannot take it any longer.

On October 5, 2005, Staff Sergeant Eddie Adamson walked out of his motel room and shot himself in the head. It was an obvious case of suicide, and the horrors in his head were laid out for all to see.

Sergeant Adamson had been on the Emergency Response Team of the Toronto Police Force back in 1980 when a robbery went bad and a fellow member of the ERT ended up as a wounded hostage. Standing outside for 90 min listening to his wounded partner beg for help, Adamson was no longer able to stomach the order to wait on negotiations. Adamson and a few others stormed the bar where Constable Michael Sweet lay dying. When the shootout was over, despite attempts by Adamson to revive him, Constable Sweet was dead.

The Price of Policing

It may seem odd that I discuss suicides and dysfunction in a chapter called "Dedicated to the Job." However, it is important to ponder what could bring a cop to the point where he would put a gun in his mouth and pull the trigger or drive a car into a Mack truck. It is in painting that picture that we truly get a sense of what cops are dedicated to when we say they are "dedicated to the job."

Detective Shane Halliday observed: "A lot of old-time cops just buried it, and it affected them in many ways, some having a morbid and dark sense of humor in order to deal with what they had seen and dealt with. There are things that I still remember as clearly as the day they happened and probably always will, and I just try not to think about them. It was all part of being a cop, the part that the public probably doesn't know about." Halliday continued, "For many years, when members completed a call of a traumatic nature, they were expected to just suck it up and get on with their job. Now they have employee assistance programs where members can talk about and deal with events." But, in spite of the help that is now available, policing is still a job that exacts a high price from those who undertake it.

The point that I am trying to get across is that police are just human beings like the rest of us. They have the same emotions, they have families and lives similar to ours, and they struggle with many of the same dysfunctions that we struggle with. Yet, even though they are just human beings like the rest of us, we expect them to do a superhuman job.

Policing is a job that requires members to see the worst of humanity and somehow react in a way that shows the best of humanity. The average starting pay for a police officer is between $50,000 and $60,000 a year, and for that we ask them to deal with insanity that we, for the most part, want to pretend does not exist. We ask them to deal with the suicides, the car crashes, the drownings, the freak accidents, the domestic disputes, and the crazy lady with a cat in the tree—and then we ask them to keep these haunting horrors to themselves. On top of all that, we want them to be role models to our children, defend justice, protect us and our property, solve addiction problems, win the war on drugs, and solve crimes. We hold them to a higher level of integrity than others in society, and when they fail our expectations, we crucify them. What is surprising is not that some of them snap, but that most of them do not.

A Picture of Dedication

Not long ago, I woke up to another horror story. It took place in Moncton, New Brunswick, where both my handler Mike Cabana and I began our careers and our work together. Briefly, this is what happened. RCMP officers Constable Fabrice Georges Gevaudan, Constable Douglas James Larche, and Constable Dave Ross were ambushed on their way to a call about a man with a weapon. They did not stand a chance, as they were shot down while the perpetrator hid in the tree line with a high-powered rifle and scope. These men had all lived a life of service to their families, friends, and community, and they all died doing what they loved. One story stands out to me that illustrates the dedication not only of these officers but of most officers that I have met over the years.

Constable Dave Ross was in his back yard, waiting for his pregnant wife Rachel to arrive home. They had celebrated their wedding anniversary just weeks before. No doubt his head was filled with joyful plans for the time they would spend together. Known among his peers as one who always wanted to be first on the scene, when the call came in, Constable Ross rushed off with his partner, Danny the police dog. Constable Ross would be first on the scene for the last time. When he arrived, he was slaughtered without mercy. When Rachael arrived home, the barbecue was still on and the garage door wide open.

Like most officers, Constable Ross did not give a second thought to dropping all that he was doing so that he could go out and protect the community in which he lived, if need be with his own life. The saddest part I see in all of this is that police officers' dedication is only recognized by the public when they die in the line of duty and not when they bring that same sense of dedication to every shift of their life.

Every shift, police officers across this country go to their briefings, check their equipment, head out to the streets, and try to live up to the expectations that are placed on them. It takes someone who is very dedicated just to be a rank and file police officer—let alone an officer who leaves the patrol car behind to specialize in some other area of policing. It is from these dedicated professionals that those who will work in the undercover world are chosen. And among those chosen are the handpicked few who are considered ready for the job of handling civilian sources.

I want to be clear. Most police officers deal with human sources, some well and some not so well. As I discussed in Section I of this book, dealing with sources is not an easy task. In Section II, I hope to give an idea of what it takes to go beyond the dedication of every officer and be an exceptionally strong handler.

Trust

8

Trust is the glue of life. It's the most essential ingredient in effective communication. It's the foundational principle that holds all relationships.

—Stephen Covey

A few years ago, I wrote a letter to Raf Souccar, who at the time was the assistant commissioner of the RCMP. It was an open letter in that it was published, in an edited and paraphrased form, in one of Canada's major newspapers by one of the country's leading crime reporters. The letter was written out of frustration at my situation and was probably a little biased. Even worse, in my opinion, the paraphrase was done in the interest of sensationalism in order to sell newspapers. I will not include the entire letter here, as I do not believe that it would serve a purpose in moving forward. However, I will include an excerpt that fits the theme of this chapter and will help lay the groundwork for Section II: "If I could use an analogy of what it's like to be a source for the RCMP, I would have to compare it to an abusive marriage. One partner has all the control, exercises it often, and does not care about the pain or hurt that the rest of the family suffers, especially the pain of the abused."

Dysfunctional or not, the relationship between an informant and the police is very much like a marriage. I touched on this in the first section of this book, but in the following pages I want to delve much deeper into the relationship. I want to show the intimacy that is required to make the relationship successful and touch on the issues that can turn the relationship toward one of abuse, dysfunction, and disaster. I want to look at what is required to make the relationship flourish and be beneficial to both participants—even if that is the most unlikely of outcomes when weighing the odds.

In every marriage, friendship, or business alliance, the key ingredient is trust. That may seem blatantly obvious. But, given the work atmosphere in which the police officer and informant usually meet, and given the violence, manipulative nature, and ingrained criminality of most informants, it would seem that trust would be nearly impossible. In fact, it would seem, based on Section I of this book, that the excerpt from my letter to Raf Souccar should be reversed, with the informant most often being the abusive partner.

Trust, as Steven Covey says, is "the foundational principle that holds all relationships." If this is true, then how can trust be achieved and maintained in this seemingly temperamental pairing? I suggest that the strength and success of the relationship depends primarily on the character of the officer. The informant might make the decision on who he will look to in order to pass on information. However, that decision is going to be based on the instinct that tells him the officer has his best interest at heart.

What quality must there be in police officers to make that trust possible? Why do some excel in this area more than others? Trustworthiness comes from both the nature and the nurture of those leading, from their inherent abilities and their training. The following quotes from RCMP deputy commissioner Mike Cabana—and the subsequent chapters—will give you an idea of what I mean:

- "Informants are people, and many of them bring significant baggage and regularly need assistance navigating through personal issues/events affecting them. A handler needs to be prepared to help to the extent possible. This is very much a two-way relationship."
- "A handler needs to remain focused on the end result while ensuring the activities of the informant do not cross the proverbial line."
- "A good handler also needs to understand that he/she is part of a much broader team and needs to be able to engage the support of other members (and sometimes people outside the organization) while ensuring the security/safety of the informant."
- "Safety of the informant needs to remain the primary focus, and a handler needs to be prepared to walk away from good information if he/she feels it may compromise the safety of the informant."
- "A good handler needs fairly strong communication skills and some degree of intellectual dexterity."
- "A good handler possesses an ability to easily observe/listen to a source and analyze what they say/don't say/exhibit in body language and read their character strengths/weaknesses and motivators. With this information, he/she can use strategies to subtly persuade and influence the person."
- "Advanced skills in interpretation can be taught, but communication skills and the ability to 'think on your feet,' so to speak, have to be there."

At age forty-nine, my current understanding of the relationship between source and handler has been developed after much introspection and soul searching. I believe that trustworthiness begins with the character of the officer, even though it may be enhanced by training. Trust begins with the officer, not so much with the informant.

All police officers have some degree of trustworthiness, or they would not be on the force. Some have earned gold stars in this area, and others are failing miserably. Some police officers are entrusted with the uniform, but not the gun. Some get to dress in the dog man's uniform, but are not given the dog. In other words, if they have been handed the team jersey, they are part of the team, but that doesn't necessarily mean that they are in the game.

In Section I of this book, I described a world filled with violence, hatred, insecurity, and greed. One would find it difficult to believe that trust could be found anywhere among those who were living that lifestyle. However, trust is sometimes found, in small amounts, in the most unlikely of places. It may be the trust between a drug dealer and a junkie that extends to a certain level of credit. It may be the trust between a bouncer and a stripper to keep peering eyes from becoming groping hands. It may be in the assurance by a partner that your family will be cared for and protected while you are in prison. Trust may be hard to find in the criminal world, but it is there. Since it is in such short supply and such high demand in that world, if you find it, you will likely hold on to it pretty tightly. And that is what an informant does when he finds the right handler, the one that he can trust—he grabs hold as tightly as he can and tries never to let him go.

First Time

The arrest had taken place at least a couple of weeks earlier, but I still had the main gun that had been used by the armed robbery suspects. It was a .410 sawed-off, pump-action shotgun. I had called Mike the next day, and when he did not answer, I had left a message. Sometimes, between his busy schedule and my crazy life, it would take some time for us to connect. I suppose I could have just given the gun to any cop, but that was not an option in my mind. I was convinced that Mike was a man of his word. I did not necessarily hold that same conviction about police officers in general.

I did finally reach Mike, and now the time had arrived. I walked slowly along the street, not far from a police station and only blocks from the city hospital. As I took each step, I became more nervous. I believed Mike when he said I could safely turn the gun over, but what about his superiors? Were they going to let me hand it off and then just leave?

An old, brown Chevy Caprice pulled up beside me, with the windows rolled down, and came to a stop. Mike spoke with a reassuring but commanding voice, telling me where to place the gun in the back seat. As quickly as he had pulled up, he pulled away, telling me to call him later.

I would call him later. In fact, I would go on calling Mike for the next thirty years. A relationship that began with his assurance that he would protect me has grown through the years. It has survived waves of darkness, deceit, death, and many other things that could have destroyed it. The secret of its strength lies with the one who is trusted, Mike the police officer.

Trust in an Unlikely Situation

The room was bright, too bright, and it seemed as if I had been in it forever. I didn't know what time it was, nor did I have a clue how long I had been in this confined space not much bigger than a bathroom. I knew the interrogation had begun shortly after 1:30 p.m. when they had placed me under arrest for murder.

I was growing weary with the bombardment of questions and accusations. I was becoming more tired of the ridiculous cat and mouse games that accompanied the questions. I felt sick to my stomach, my head was aching, and I just wanted to close my eyes so all of this would disappear. Everything in me said I should give up so I could rest. Everyone else in the room was working toward that same end. The problem was not whether I should tell the truth about what had happened. The question was who I should tell it to. I was facing very serious consequences, and I didn't know who I could trust. Should I accept the assurances of the officer who was handling the good guy routine, place my confidence in the guy doing the bad cop routine, or have faith in the one who was neutral?

Looking back fifteen years later, I see that I had to trust each of them to some degree. In fact, after I struck a deal and agreed to wear a wire so that all the other people involved in the murder could be captured and proven guilty, I would have to trust the one I liked the least more often than I wanted.

Detective Shane Halliday, one of the cops involved, has stated, "In order for any operation to succeed, there must be trust." It still leaves me dumbfounded today that either side was ever able to trust in that situation. As I look back, it amazes me how that trust was ever sustained, with me trying so hard to undermine it.

It seems as if it would be impossible to trust in such a situation. After all, a police officer is meant to uphold the law, to be a pillar in the community, to be an example to others of what is right and to be willing to sacrifice himself for the good of the community in which he serves. On the other hand, the informant is more often than not exactly the opposite—self-centered, manipulative, rebellious, and habituated to acting contrary to the laws of society. How do these two come together, trust one another for the good, and not have it turn out badly? It is simple in theory but not so easy in practice. The light of good in the police officer must be stronger than the darkness in the informant. It is a constant battle, and whichever one is stronger will control the relationship. Max Depree says, "Earning trust is not easy, nor is it cheap, nor does it happen quickly. Earning trust is hard and demanding work. Trust comes only with genuine effort, never with a lick and a promise."

Trusting with My Life on the Line

I was standing at the bar trying to have a conversation with Hells Angel Neil Smith. After all, that was the objective of the meet. I was wearing a hidden wire while a cover team kept an eye on things from outside the building. The dialogue between Neil and me was just starting to pick up when my phone rang. It was Fridge (Officer Steve Murray) telling me that I should get the hell out of there. As an officer doing surveillance outside, he was uncomfortable with the arrival of unexpected guests. I pretended it was my woman on the phone, said I would be home soon and then hung up.

In walked Wayne and Bobby, both killers, who had just reconciled after a dispute that had almost seen one take out the other. I understood why Fridge would perceive their arrival as a threat and signal me to get out, since the dispute that had taken place had revolved around their partnerships with me. From the outside, it might have looked as if they were there to kill me. The phone rang again. Fridge again told me to get out, adding that the operation was over and the police were "shutting it down." I responded once again as if he was my girlfriend, saying that I was busy and I would be home when I got there. It was getting tense at this point but not because of any danger from the inside. It was getting dangerous because of the odd calls that were coming from my supposed girlfriend. The three killers standing around me knew that my woman would never harass me while I was doing business, so the phone calls were very much out of the norm.

Wayne called me aside to talk privately. Although I was a little tense, I was not overly suspicious and went with him to a corner of the club. Thank God that I did, because Fridge called again and demanded that I leave. I barked back as if it was my girlfriend, saying that I would damn well be home when I got there. Then I angrily shut off my cell phone. It would not have been good if I had still been standing beside Neil. That would have been the third call that I had received in front of him, and that would have been completely out of character.

I finished up inside and waited for the safest opportunity to get out the door and meet up with the cover team. When I was safely outside and walking toward the meet area, I turned the phone back on so I could voice my anger toward Fridge for not trusting my judgment. I was livid that he thought he knew better than I did. How could he possibly know if it was safe for me to leave? I did not get to unleash the barrage of thoughts I had stored up for him because just as I was about to dial the number, Shane pulled up and told me to get into his vehicle.

I repeat once more what was said by Shane Halliday, the detective, now retired, who was running that operation: "In order for any operation to succeed, there must be trust."

The Need for Trust

I have given three examples of the need for trust. In the first story, I trusted Mike Cabana enough to voluntarily hand over a potential murder weapon. In the second story, my back was against the wall, and I needed to know when to break and hand over information that I knew could incriminate me. In the last story, I had to trust police officers in the midst of an operation in which my life was at stake.

In all three examples, I had handlers who were dealing with me. But only in the first one did I really trust that the officer had my best interest at heart. In the following chapters, I will describe the other characteristics of a strong handler, the other qualities that convinced me I could trust the police officer I was dealing with.

Empathy 9

Human morality is unthinkable without empathy.

—**Frans de Waal**

Empathy is defined in the dictionary not as sympathy, although many understand it in that way; rather, it is the feeling that you understand and share another person's experiences and emotions. I believe empathy can be summed up in the answer I received from Mike Cabana when I asked him what characteristics he thought made him a good handler: "You had to understand that we do not all have the same lot in life, and I felt that I had a responsibility to help those who helped me." Mike also emphasized fairness: "Regardless of how much I sympathized with the personal situation of some of the people I was dealing with, it was important to remain fair to everyone and not to be making exceptions or turning a blind eye."

Empathy is very closely connected to humility. An officer needs to understand the concept of "There, but for the grace of God, go I." If he cannot understand this, how can that officer think anything other than that he is better than the person he is dealing with?

I have already outlined how trust and empathy go hand in hand to form better communication and better relationships. Let's take it a little further. Almost everyone has some form of empathy, but there are also degrees or levels of empathy. The three levels are

1. *Intellectually*: We know with our brain what someone may be experiencing or feeling
2. *Emotionally*: We can feel the experience of someone
3. *Responsively*: We want to do something that can help that person's situation

I believe that trust and trusted relationships have their foundation in these three levels of empathy. A strong handler will have all three, including a responsive empathy. In contrast, a weak handler is likely to have only an intellectual or theoretical grasp of empathy. This will result in a lack of humility and offer a very weak foundation for a trusting relationship.

An Example

Detective Shane Halliday observed, "The handler must not put himself above the agent and must show empathy."

Shane undercover in 1986 during an organized crime operation

As I followed the unmarked police car in front of me, I could not help but wonder: Was it me who was insane, or was it the driver leading me to the police station who was nuts? Shane Halliday was a tall man who looked very intimidating. As a senior homicide detective, he had convinced me to follow him to the police station so that for the second time in a week I could be placed under arrest for murder. One of us had to be crazy. It was either me for not running or Shane for trusting me not to run.

Today it is easy to see why I followed Shane: I trusted him. I have already talked about the importance of trust. I debated for a long time whether that should be the first or the last characteristic of a good handler that I should discuss. Why is that? For the very simple reason that trust is a result of all the other characteristics that make a good cop a great cop. In the context of this book, it's the difference between an officer controlling his source and the source controlling the officer.

Shane sporting a beard for photo ID in 2001

Thinking back on that particular day brings to mind something that was crucial to the eventual success that Shane had in dealing with me. When I walked into the interrogation room on both occasions, I was the one who knew the truth regarding the murder and all that surrounded it. The police had ideas, thoughts, opinions, and bits of information, but certainly not the truth. Each time an officer came in and insisted he knew what had happened, outlining the scenario he thought was most likely, the easier it became for me to see which cops were playing which role. It allowed me to see who was authentic and who was not. At the end of the ordeal, it was the authenticity and genuineness of Shane Halliday and an officer named Greg Mason that convinced me I could trust them. It did not seem that they were trying to do anything other than put themselves in my shoes and empathize with me while being true to their responsibilities. Looking back, it seems clear to me that Greg was displaying an emotional empathy and Shane was displaying all three. Why did this matter? It was their ability to authentically care for people that made me trust them and eventually help solve the murder. It was because I believed they had everyone's best interest at heart.

I have thought a long time about what to say about Sergeant Steve Murray, who was affectionately nicknamed "Fridge." In a documentary made about this case, he stated, "We were going to have to make a deal with the devil." I mention this because Steve was somewhat of an exception to the rule of empathy. I believe that Steve made a terrible handler in regards to dealing with informants. I have a number of reasons for thinking that, but it is also possible that I have a somewhat biased opinion on the matter. I don't think so, but that is a possibility. I also know that during my time with him he was under a lot of personal stress.

The reason I bring this up is that, although Steve had only an intellectual empathy for me at best, that was not the case with the victim's family. Steve had to deal with the family of Sean Simmons, the victim of the murder, and then had to come and deal with me, an informant and also a participant in the murder. I may not have seen any care for my well-being in him, but the three degrees of empathy that he showed toward the victim's family were so overwhelming that it was easy for me to look past his opinion of me and trust him on a much different level; deep down, it was almost as if I empathized with the victim's family and their grief vicariously through him. In that sense, I am glad he was there, even though I was convinced he was a danger to the operation because of his lack of empathy and other critical characteristics of a good handler.

Training

Neil deGrasse Tyson wrote, "Humans aren't as good as we should be in our capacity to empathize with feelings and thoughts of others, be they humans or other animals on Earth. So maybe part of our formal education should be training in empathy. Imagine how different the world would be if, in fact, that were 'reading, writing, arithmetic, empathy'." I believe what Tyson wrote to be true. If what he suggests were put into effect, I believe the world would look much different today than it does. Although that is unlikely to ever happen, it is not unrealistic to think that this teaching could be implemented on a much deeper level in basic police training, especially in regards to source handling.

If I were to rewrite the quote to fit this book more specifically, it would be like this: "Police officers aren't all as good as they could be in their capacity to empathize with feelings and thoughts of informants. So maybe part of their preparation to become police officers should be training in empathy. Imagine how different their world would be if, in fact, that were 'defensive driving, report writing, target practice, and empathy'."

Another Example

Again I want to emphasize that empathy is not sympathy. I also want to share one more story that highlights the way I have seen Mike Cabana temper his empathy for an informant with the fairness and responsibility of his duty.

It was midsummer of 1992, and I was sitting in a jail in Eastern Canada. My nine-month sentence was almost over, and I was looking forward to being released to the area where Mike was stationed. It was my hope that, through the connections I had made during my incarceration, I would have plenty of information to pass on to him.

One Saturday night, I was at a weekly seven-step spiritual program for addictions when I was called to the phone at the main office. It was the mother of my first two children, claiming she had been threatened by two gang members because of my work for the RCMP. Unfortunately for Mike, everything is intensified and a lot more dramatic when informants are sitting helpless in a jail cell rather than being able to take action on issues like these themselves.

It took until the next morning for me to actually be able to speak to Mike directly, after playing phone tag through guards at the jail and secretaries at the detachment. When we finally did talk, I exploded with concern, worry, and demands, while Mike responded with his usual calm demeanor. I remember him assuring me he would do all he could to look into the situation, telling me not to worry about it and promising that he would have someone watch the house while things were figured out. The call lasted only as long as it took for Mike to assure me that he would do all that he could. I was still helpless, but I went back to my cell feeling a little less stressed.

As radio host Paul Harvey used to say, "And now for the rest of the story." I am sitting here twenty-two years later reading the report Mike submitted regarding that incident. The beginning of the report summed up what I had told him on the phone. It went on to discuss my manipulative track record and the likelihood of threats actually having been made toward my girlfriend. In the report, Mike also commented positively on my work as an informant and an agent. The first paragraph contained the following: "This member has been involved with this source for a number of years and has come to know him very well. It is this member's opinion that J-1028 either fabricated or inflated the existence of these threats hoping to gain an early release." The last sentence of the report was "This writer is fully aware of source's capabilities and character traits and always approaches him cautiously."

This incident highlights many of the traits I have come to admire in strong handlers, including the balance between empathy and duty. Mike was right that the threats were likely fabricated, although not by me; in hindsight, I think the information I received may not have been true. The seriousness of the threats was absolutely inflated by me, exactly as Mike said and for the reasons he gave. But the report went on to say that, regardless of his opinion, Mike still had someone watch my girlfriend's house and investigate the threat.

I can tell you that, twenty-two years later, Mike will still assess cautiously, reassure authentically, act professionally, and call a spade a spade. The same is true for the other police officers I deemed to be strong handlers.

Caught, Not Taught

Matthieu Ricard wrote, "Neuroscience has proven that similar areas of the brain are activated both in the person who suffers and in the one who feels empathy. Thus, empathic suffering is a true experience of suffering." I started this chapter by saying that sympathy and empathy are different. Sympathy is someone trying his or her best to relate to your experience and feel for you in it. Empathy is someone having the ability to put himself or herself inside you and experience your reality.

I believe that empathy is not something that can be taught but rather something that has to be caught. It has to be real and natural in order to be perceived as authentic. Empathy cannot be faked, while sympathy is very often a façade. If it was me making the decisions—and it surely is not—I would have the screening process for all police officers include looking for those who have the natural ability to empathize. I would then spend the resources necessary to train those officers to work with both victims and informants.

There is a reason that I cry every time I watch a police funeral. It's not because I am sad about death. I cry when someone graduates. I am sad when someone is charged with a crime. My adrenaline flows when a police car flies down the road with or without the siren blaring. Empathy allows me to get inside another person and experience what that person is experiencing. I rarely sympathize.

Understanding Motives 10

Actions are visible, though motives are secret.

—**Samuel Johnson**

An informant is the arms, legs, and eyes of a handler. As an informant, understanding other people's motives was crucial to my survival. For handlers, understanding an informant's motives is crucial for the survival of the operation and of everyone involved in it. Therefore, a handler must try to understand the motive—or the many motives—that may lie deep in the heart of the informant. Unfortunately, sometimes this is not possible. Sometimes the handler will have to make judgment calls about unseen motives, based on visible actions.

A Good Day to Die

I did not know the informant I am about to discuss, but I have known many criminals just like him. I understand a bit about Cory Patterson's story, first, because I walked the same informant walk he was walking, and second, because I have dealt with—and helped take down—psychopaths just like him.

Cory Patterson was first coded as a source for the RCMP in November of 1990. He was known in organized crime circles as an enforcer, someone who collected debts and enjoyed doing it. He had the nickname "Rambo" due to his usual attire (military style clothing), his mercenary abilities, and his knowledge of weapons. Patterson's career has been chronicled in a thoroughly researched story called "Killer Cory" written by crime writer Gary Dimmock. It clearly paints a picture of an informant who, in my opinion, should not have been used. And, if a case warranted him being used, he was an agent who needed a very strong handler.

The target of Patterson's biggest undercover operation, code-named Project Ice, was a longtime friend named Paul ("Sunny") Braybrook. Braybrook, then sergeant-at-arms of the Toronto outlaw motorcycle gang Para-Dice Riders, had hired Patterson to collect drug debts. After being accepted as an informant, Patterson introduced a veteran RCMP undercover corporal to members of the Para-Dice Riders. Patterson continued to buy drugs and accept assignments as a hired gun while the undercover police officer collected evidence.

In mass raids on April 15, 1993, RCMP and Ontario Provincial Police officers arrested forty suspects, including Paul Braybrook, and seized thousands of dollars worth of crack cocaine, LSD, hashish, marijuana, angel dust, and weapons.

In an August 13, 1993, agent assessment, another corporal with the Barrie Joint Forces Drug Squad wrote that Patterson "did not perform well unless closely supervised... O-3498 required almost continuous supervision in order to maintain any measure of motivation." However, he also reported that the RCMP had no concerns about retaining Patterson as a source.

Since Patterson's cover had been blown in Ontario, the RCMP relocated him and his common-law wife, a crack cocaine addict, to Halifax, Nova Scotia. The Mounties also paid off $10,000 Patterson had racked up in credit card debts. On May 7, 1994, Patterson and his wife got into an argument over drugs, and a shotgun went off. No one was hurt, they gave conflicting stories to police about the incident, and Patterson was charged with assault causing bodily harm and dangerous storage of a firearm. In jail, he went berserk, screaming that he'd kill a police officer or guard. The police had to pepper spray him to get him under control.

In an "urgent" memo dated May 10, 1994, a Halifax RCMP inspector said Patterson was "cracked out," "very aggressive," and a "loose cannon." The RCMP believed Patterson was abusing prescription painkillers and was on the "quick road to exploding." However, Patterson denied he had a drug problem. At least one Halifax RCMP officer thought that the only way to find out if he was telling the truth was to place him in a detox program.

Meanwhile, Patterson had made an insurance claim on a $15,000 ring he claimed had been stolen. Insurance company investigator Steve Zacher, a former Dartmouth police officer, ran a computer check on Patterson. He told the RCMP about his investigation since he had discovered that Patterson was in the Force's Witness Protection Program. The insurance company refused to pay the claim, Patterson threatened to sue, and the RCMP ended up paying Patterson $9,500 for his alleged insurance claim.

In spring 1994, the RCMP bought Patterson's common-law wife a one-way ticket out of town and relocated Patterson to Fredericton, New Brunswick. An RCMP memo stated, "O-3498 refused to enter the detox program stating that he didn't have a problem; however, his behaviors and mannerisms indicated otherwise." Nevertheless, the RCMP gave Patterson a new undercover assignment infiltrating drug traffickers in Fredericton. An agreement signed on January 20, 1995, gave Patterson a salary, expenses, and the promise of a $5,000 reward at the end of the operation.

Patterson was also still testifying in the trials of those arrested back in Ontario. During the trial of Willard Low-On, the accused said that, during the time Patterson was a police informant, Patterson had shoved a gun in his face and threatened his life if he didn't give Patterson drugs and lease him a restaurant. Low-On's lawyer also questioned Patterson about the death of sixteen-year-old John Paul Lapham, who had overdosed in Patterson's house in 1992.

Low-On was convicted of drug trafficking on January 3, 1995. However, after the trial, Justice Paul Hermiston was highly critical of the RCMP decision to use Patterson as an informant. Hermiston described Patterson as "a devious criminal who has been able to manipulate the Royal Canadian Mounted Police into thinking that he has turned over a new leaf...He has hoodwinked the authorities. His testimony is completely unreliable." Hermiston also recommended that Patterson be investigated regarding Lapham's death and regarding welfare fraud, since Patterson had admitted under oath that he had been collecting welfare while on the RCMP payroll.

Instead of investigating, the RCMP asked Patterson why the judge was so biased against him. In a March 1, 1995 memo, a corporal with New Brunswick's J Division reported Patterson's answer: "Years ago, the judge was a lawyer in the same law firm which represented J-1483 [Patterson] in his divorce. The judge had heard J-1483 discussing his case with his lawyer and interrupted the conversation to tell both J-1483 and the lawyer that he found J-1483's views to be 'repugnant.'" Patterson also said that the judge was dissatisfied with a reclining chair he had bought from a furniture shop owned by Patterson's father.

The trial of "Sunny" Braybrook on cocaine and weapons charges followed a few months later, and Braybrook chose to defend himself. During Braybrook's cross-examination of Patterson, the informant admitted he had collected welfare illegally and had given false information to his parole supervisor. Further, Braybrook demonstrated that Patterson was lying on a number of other issues and that Patterson's notes for the RCMP were full of errors. Braybrook also accused Patterson of continuing to commit crimes and of continuing to abuse drugs and alcohol while being an informant. Most seriously, Braybrook questioned Patterson about John Paul Lapham.

Braybrook was convinced Patterson had killed Lapham by giving him a massive morphine overdose on August 8, 1992. A police news release had said that only Patterson and his girlfriend had been in the house with Lapham at the time. However, crime writer Gary Dimmock later discovered evidence that others had also been present. After Lapham collapsed, Patterson had apparently ordered the others to leave, removed all drugs from the house and waited several hours before finally calling the police.

On November 3, 1995, Department of Justice officials and police met and decided to drop all charges against Braybrook and the remaining Project Ice defendants—largely because of their informant's lack of credibility on the witness stand.

Patterson's further career as an informant led to no more convictions and soon fell apart as a result of numerous problems. During his undercover work in J Division, police found another body in the basement suite of the house he was living in. Patterson's career finally ended in death. He was found with a note pinned to his chest saying that it was a good day to die. Patterson had overdosed on drugs and had been shot through the head with a flare gun.

Evaluating Informants

Winston Churchill said, "True genius resides in the capacity for evaluation of uncertain, hazardous, and conflicting information."

In Section I of this book, I discussed the many motives informants have for risking their lives by giving information to the police. Many of those motives have to do with their need to survive in the criminal world and the greedy desire to fill their pockets. It is obviously important for handlers to understand those motives if they want to utilize a source in a way that is productive and safe. I believe most officers dealing with informants understand these motives and take them into account. However, the strongest handlers are those who have the ability to evaluate uncertain, hazardous, and conflicting information even when the source does not seem to have a clear motive.

What can be gleaned from the story of Cory Patterson in regards to understanding an informant's motives? Hindsight is always 20/20, but my first thoughts when hearing Patterson's history focused on the statements, "In jail, he went berserk, screaming that he'd kill a police officer or guard. The police had to pepper spray him." I understand many aspects of Patterson's behavior—the drug use, the manipulation, the rocky relationship, the power trips, and the bragging. I can even empathize with him when they put him in jail after the shotgun incident—I have been in that particular jail, and I have been there while I was in a very volatile relationship. What I cannot wrap my mind around is the actual violence that was so much a part of everything Patterson did, as opposed to the practice of most informants to play the role of being dangerous. That, mixed with the threat mentioned above to kill a member of law enforcement, would have been enough for most officers I know to stop dealing with him and reassess the motives on both sides.

It is not that there are not ways to deal with sources such as Cory Patterson. However, the resources required and the risk involved when dealing with extremely screwed-up informants is an indication that they should only be used in extreme cases such as the solving of murders, kidnappings, and crimes of severe violence.

Looking Within

William Godwin said, "The philosophy of the wisest man that ever existed is mainly derived from the act of introspection."

I have talked about the importance of handlers understanding the motives of an informant and how crucial that is to an operation's success. It is even more important for handlers to understand their own motives. What was the return on the investment in Cory Patterson? Were the targets worth the risk of continuing to use him? At what point should a handler look inside himself and decide to tell his superiors that it's time to cut an informant loose?

As I look back and consider all of the police officers I have dealt with over the past few decades, I see that there were many common threads in the good ones and the not so good ones. By far, the most common thread among the good ones was the ability to look within and examine their own motives. There is no doubt that every human being should do this. Surely everyone who joins a police force should do it. But for an officer who becomes one with a criminal, serving as a handler for a criminal informant, it is essential to remain introspective every minute of every day.

Clear and Concise Communication

11

The single biggest problem in communication is the illusion that it has taken place.

—George Bernard Shaw

In a memo dated November 6, 1992, Inspector Connolly of J Division wrote the following assessment of me as a police informant:

> The fact that his agent status had previously terminated was fully explained. Also, the importance of confidentiality was discussed, and J-1028 was directed to concentrate on improving his track record in this regard. Furthermore, it was stressed that any future relationship with the Force as a human source was possible only on a very professional basis. Considering the foregoing, J-1028 was advised that he could pass on any information he felt would be of further interest to the Force. Furthermore, upon being released from jail, J-1028 advised Cst. J.G.P. Cabana that he intends to reside in the Fredericton, N.B., area with his family. Considering the foregoing, it is recommended that Cst. Cabana be designated the main handler of this source and that a co-handler be identified from Fredericton Detachment personnel. Should J-1028 relocate to the Moncton area, it is suggested that an experienced source handler be identified by OC Moncton Sub/Division.

This brief memo invokes a very vivid memory for me every time I read it. I was being housed in a county jail not far from the detachment where Mike Cabana was now stationed. It was my intention to move to that area when released and continue to pass information on as an informant, with the hope that it would lead to another operation as an agent. During my stay at the jail, I was communicating back and forth with Mike, even though there was a danger that it could disclose my relationship with the Force and therefore compromise my safety.

I remember sitting in a small office area waiting for Mike. I knew he was coming to see me about the insecure communications, but I had no idea he was bringing company. I felt a bit of fear when he and two older, plainclothed guys came into the cramped area. I was uncomfortable with the fact that it would be three smart cops against one narcissistic, know-it-all informant. It was highly unlikely that I would be doing much talking, let alone manipulating the conversation.

Mike introduced the two officers, and then he stepped back and let them take over. I tried to keep my eyes focused, staring them down, as they very assertively made each of their points. I don't remember how well I did at that, but I do know that that twenty-minute reality check seemed to go on for hours. Then it ended as abruptly as it began and the two other men were gone, leaving Mike and me in a very quiet, tension-filled room.

It was not me who broke the silence. I was still speechless, trying to restore my wounded pride. Mike then went over each point:

- My agent status was for the length of time specified in the Letter of Agreement we had signed, and all of the benefits of that status had ended when the operation ended.
- Passing letters addressed to Mike to select guards at the jail was a risk and could compromise my security.
- Making phone calls through those same guards was also a risk.
- Until I was released from jail, the risk was too great for me to risk passing on information.
- I should contact Mike when I was released, and it would be decided then if I would work again.

I remember every minute of that experience, which was well over twenty years ago, due to one reason: the communication was very clear and concise. The fact is that I don't believe Mike needed the two guys with him because his communication skills were always good. Even though I don't remember everything he ever spoke to me, I remember perfectly every time he raised his voice a little, because his voice commanded attention.

The point I am getting at is this: As an informant, I might have heard and even understood everything that was said to me, but, like a rebellious kid, I was always going to try to push the boundaries. Over the years, Mike perfected the skill of knowing when to let me "debrief" and when to be assertive. This was invaluable in making my chaotic world mesh with his.

Getting Through

Sydney J. Harris said, "The two words 'information' and 'communication' are often used interchangeably, but they signify quite different things. Information is giving out; communication is getting through."

In the meeting I just described, Mike needed to make me aware of the risk I was taking, warning me that it could end my work as an informant and even possibly my life. In this next example, I risked not only my own life but also the lives of all of those working with me, not to mention the time and money that had already been invested in the operation.

It was near the end of Operation Download, and the stress level for everyone was very high. I had spent the last few months living under a microscope. My house was wired, my cell phone was wired, and almost every time I left the house I was wearing a wire. The Hells Angels were growing weary with my excuses for not making the same money I had been making before the operation and a little suspicious of me always bringing up the murder that was being investigated.

My girlfriend Tina and I left for the private club that Hells Angel Neil Smith ran his operations out of. It was a pretty typical afternoon. I was wearing a wire and feeling the pressure of needing to get some good "intercepts," some criminal admissions on tape.

Neil was not there when we arrived, but Bobby Milton was. He came straight over to meet me at the bar, probably so he could put his drinks on my tab as usual. Bobby was an ex-member of the Hells Angels who still did a lot of their dirty work. He had partnered with me in previous months.

Bobby and I were standing there talking when Neil finally showed up. He walked toward the bar, grabbed a beer, and motioned for me to follow him upstairs. I grabbed my drink and went up behind him to the most restricted area of the club. It was the second level, and only those who did direct business with the Hells Angels were allowed up there. Neil came up close to me, with his head next to mine and only inches above the microphones that were concealed beneath my sweater. I was sweating bullets as he began telling me that he wanted to know what was going on with some of the others who had participated in the murder that he had ordered. The discussion lasted only a few minutes, but I was excited and scared to death all at the same time. I believed I had finally gotten what was needed to convict Neil. Unfortunately, days later, I would find out that because he mumbled so much and talked with such a quiet voice, we did not capture everything he had said.

It may have been disappointing days later, but that afternoon I was pumped. I came out of the club to meet the cover team on such an adrenaline high that I could hardly contain myself. The cover team was also happy and wanted to get back and immediately listen to the intercepts. It was decided that I could wait until the next morning at the safe house to write my notes. Being my usual manipulative self, I decided to ask them to give Tina and me our weekly pay early and drop us off at another Hells Angels–run pool hall so we could celebrate with supper and a few drinks.

After a bit, they agreed to pay us early and let us have a night out—and it ended in disaster. The only stipulation they had made was that we not get into any trouble, yet, that is precisely what we did. After too many drinks, we were heading home in a taxi when Tina asked to stop at a certain store. We had once lived above the store, and Tina was still angry with the owner because she believed he had kept a lot of our belongings when we had moved. When she lost her temper and went over the counter to get to the owner, one of the employees pressed the holdup alarm. In a matter of minutes, the store was surrounded with police, and we were in the trouble we had been asked to avoid.

Thankfully, when our names were radioed in, the matter was quickly dealt with by investigators. A patrol officer handcuffed us and put us in her car as if we were under arrest and whisked us away. I say "thankfully," but when the officer dropped us off at our house, I have to admit I was not feeling thankful, thinking about the meeting that I knew would be inescapable the next morning.

I woke up hungover and was not feeling much like dealing with the confrontation that was about to happen. When the phone rang and I was told to get to the safe house, I was more than nervous. I knew that the night before had raised a lot of issues and risked the whole operation. However, ever the manipulator, I went into the meeting on the offensive. I walked to the parking lot of the safe house and watched as three cars carrying five investigators began to systematically and covertly empty into the building. Only Shane and I were left in the parking lot, and he was not exiting the vehicle. This was a clear indication of the type of meeting this was going to be—my main handler for the operation was not going to be attending.

I went straight to the car, opened the door and, as angrily as I could in my hungover state, told Shane that I was quitting, that the operation was done, that I had had enough, and that I was finished. I then turned and started walking away. Shane called the others over the radio and very nervously, not wanting to cause a scene and draw heat, asked me to get into the car. The others were now at the door, and I did exactly what I knew they did not want. I continued to cause a scene, saying that I was done and telling them what they could do with their operation.

What is the point of this story? What does it have to do with clear and concise communication?

This was the breaking point in a relationship that had been seriously lacking in communication. It had always been very clear what was expected of me. However, it seemed that information was only flowing one way—up the line to those making the decisions.

Don't get me wrong. I was the one who put the operation at risk. It was my decisions that were wrong both the night before and that morning. I should not have allowed us to drink that much, and I should not have allowed the taxi to stop on the way home. I also should not have gone on the offensive in the morning in an attempt to shift responsibility and blame. All of these things risked exposing my role and could have led to someone getting killed.

But, in the meetings that followed, there was true communication. Both sides sat down and shared concerns and expectations. It was no longer just orders coming down and information going back up, only to land on deaf ears. Those at the top began to take the stress we were under a little more seriously. We agreed not to drink anymore, other than the few drinks at meets with targets. They agreed to get us a membership at a gym. We agreed to stay in our wired apartment except for meets until the operation ended. They agreed to rent a hotel room for a weekend once in a while so we could be alone without our every word being recorded. Both sides communicated properly from that point on. As a result, the operation had no further problems and ended in success.

Technically, this should have been the shortest chapter. I should have just driven home the point that both Mike Cabana and Shane Halliday were almost always very clear and concise in their communication with me. The problem was with the communication going the other way. Mike and Shane had to take my jumbled thoughts and crazed actions, distill them into useful information, and communicate it to those above them. And they had to do it in a way that would satisfy my needs, would meet the objectives of their superiors and, most importantly, would not reflect negatively on the justice system. That would not be an easy task for the best of communicators.

Control and Humility 12

I have three precious things which I hold fast and prize. The first is gentleness; the second is frugality; the third is humility, which keeps me from putting myself before others. Be gentle and you can be bold; be frugal and you can be liberal; avoid putting yourself before others and you can become a leader among men.

—Lao-Tzu

A good friend of mine once quoted an Afghan proverb to me: "If you are leading and no one is following you, then you're only taking a walk." There were many reasons why I risked my life to gather information and stay loyal to Mike Cabana. There were many reasons why I listened to the directions of Shane Halliday. I have gone above and beyond expectations for both at different times and would do so today with even more conviction. When I was asked to wear a wire to a meet with a Hells Angels target who had ordered my death three days earlier, it was my trust in Shane that convinced me to take the assignment. When I was asked to stay in a car while the high-risk takedown of two violent escaped convicts took place, it was my faith in Mike that convinced me to stay. The most crucial characteristic that swayed my decision to follow these men to the degree that I did was that they understood the meaning of humility. This attitude was expressed consistently through their actions and decisions. Mike and Shane have very different personalities, but they had this characteristic in common.

Dwight D. Eisenhower said, "Humility must always be the portion of any man who receives acclaim earned in the blood of his followers and the sacrifices of his friends." I can say unequivocally that no informant will follow someone with a big ego. An informant might give information to such a person for a time for the sake of personal gain. But that is not "following"; that is "using." There are many police officers who are being used and getting played. Why is this? It is because of their inability to recognize how fine the line is between "them" and "us." It is due to their failure to see past their own importance. There are a lot of officers who think they are cultivating and leading informants when they are just taking a walk.

Observation Post

Marilyn vos Savant has said, "To acquire knowledge, one must study; but to acquire wisdom, one must observe." Prison was an interesting place to observe both police officers and criminals and their interaction with one another.

The best way to describe prison to someone who has never been in one is to use a comparison. A penitentiary can very easily be seen as a small town—but a small town with a big wall around it to keep the inhabitants from leaving. The guards, who act as the police, do not control this town as much as they oversee it from within and from the gun towers above. Their job is to keep order in a place that is often referred to by inmates as "the jungle." The criminals outnumber the guards and run the prison. There is an inmate committee that acts as the town hall, with the inmates voting to elect both the chairman/mayor and the town council. The inmates go to work every day. To serve those who live there, there is a gym, a library, a hobby shop, and an exercise track at least a quarter-mile long. If it is the right kind of prison, there may also be a hockey rink, a baseball diamond, or even tennis courts. In addition, this town has its own investigation units, court system, and jails, which are designed to maintain order, as well as gain information that can be passed to outside police forces.

What I am trying to say is that prison simulates society in many ways and is therefore a great place to observe human interactions in general. It is an especially useful place for anyone who wants to observe the mentalities and characteristics of two specific groups: criminals and police. And, obviously, where there are criminals and police, there are informants and handlers. What makes prison such a great place to observe these two groups is that, while there are a few other inhabitants, such as those who work with the convicts in hopes of rehabilitating them, for the most part the only people there are the police and those who are being policed.

My perspective comes from the interactions I observed when I was an inmate living in the jungle, from my experiences when I was an informant working within the system, and from reviewing the internal documents relating to me during the time I was incarcerated. What did I learn?

The first thing I learned from observing the interactions among guards and inmates was that, if it weren't for their different clothing, it would have been very difficult to tell the guards from the inmates. Over and over again, I saw both the depravity and the humanity of man in both groups. The American Psychological Association noted in 2009 that "although human behavior is almost always a function of the interaction of person and situation," there has been a tendency among both psychologists and the general public to overestimate "the importance of dispositional factors while underestimating situational factors." In other words, the situation they are in greatly influences people's behavior. This is not to say that the guards and inmates—or police and informants—are alike in all ways. What I am saying is that when thrown together in an environment like "the jungle" or the cold, bloody streets of the crime world, you can be sure that all will exhibit traits and actions that are good, bad, and ugly.

In many prisons, it is considered justifiable to kill any inmate who is caught talking to a guard without a sufficient reason—and such reasons are few. As you can imagine, because of this rule, there is a lot of posturing on both sides, and many times interaction results in confrontation. It was interesting to witness these confrontations and see what characteristics emerged from both sides.

A Personal Example

Looking back, what has captured my attention in the past couple of years is the confrontations I was involved in personally. I have examined how the guards responded to my behavior and, even more importantly, how I myself behaved. One incident in particular confirmed the wisdom of Saint Augustine: "It was pride that changed angels into devils; it is humility that makes men as angels."

I had been locked up in segregation in a six-by-nine cell and was becoming more claustrophobic as the days blended together. I was awaiting a decision from the warden. Part of his job was to oversee the prison's "kangaroo court" as it was called by inmates and to make the final decision on each case. After almost three months, the decision finally arrived at my cell; it was that I would be transferred immediately to a maximum security prison. I was far from happy. I would now be four hours farther away from my family and in a prison with a lot fewer privileges.

The next step was familiar to me since I had already been transferred three times in less than two years. Sometime in the next day or two, I would be handcuffed, shackled, and put on the first available prison bus. I was angry, frustrated, and determined not to oblige in any way. In fact, quite the opposite. I began acting out my anger by smashing things and screaming threats at the guards, warning them that they wouldn't be taking me out of there without a fight.

I was pacing back and forth in my cell when two guards showed up and told me to pack my gear because it was time to go. I reiterated that I would not be going without a fight. The words of a Kris Kristofferson song kept ringing in my head: "Freedom's just another word for nothing left to lose." I angrily asked the guards which one of them wanted to come through the door and make it happen. Neither guard paid much attention; instead, they just headed back to the control booth, where they could be heard calling for a cell extraction team. This was the equivalent to calling an Emergency Response Team in the outside world. One thing seemed certain—there was going to be a confrontation.

The rest of the inmates started hollering and smashing things, as a collective mentality took over the range. My anger seemed contagious, and tempers began to boil. I was at the back of my cell with a pen in each hand, and my anger was not the only thing heating up. On my desk was a hot plate with water that was just reaching a boil.

The two guards now came back to the front of my cell and asked me once more to pack my stuff. At this point, my pride was being fueled by the cheering from the rest of the range, and that was what made me hold my position. It was certainly not because I wanted to hurt anyone, and it was not because I wanted to be hurt myself. I was scared to death. But that did not stop me from continuing with the threats. I insinuated that the first guard through the door was going to wear the boiling water or have a pen lodged in the side of his head.

The extraction team was awaiting orders only five or six hundred feet away. But then the cheering started to subside. The sound of one person walking down the range was silencing each cell that was passed. The person walking down the range with such a commanding presence was a guard we all nicknamed Don Cherry, after the NHL sportscaster. Don stood at my cell door and asked me what was going on that had caused me to be so angry that day.

I know I said earlier that speaking with a guard was grounds to be killed, and that is very true. However, there is an exception to every rule. Don had been working the segregation unit for as long as anyone there could remember and was close to retirement. Everyone had a lot of respect for him, and it was very rare that anything would be said if an inmate was seen talking to him, especially while in segregation. Why was that? It was his humility and kindness. At Christmas and on other holidays, he would pack an extra big lunch on each of his shifts. Don would then share it with different guys while talking to them about their futures or their pasts. The other guards gave him a hard time about being an "inmate lover." It's sad that he was given that label just for taking time to show the inmates that he was not above them and that he was willing to listen to them.

It would be wrong to mistake meekness for weakness. Don would put a man to the ground just as quickly as the next guy. It was just that with him this was a last resort, not a first choice, and it would not be done with any pleasure. It was for these reasons—and the fact that I was looking for an out—that Don was able to defuse the situation. Don's reputation allowed me to save some respect among the inmates, as I allowed him to handcuff me and walk me to the waiting bus.

The Other Side of the Story

Prison was one of the more interesting places to be used as a source. It was also one of the most dangerous environments I ever worked in. Why was it so dangerous? The obvious answer is the violent people there and the environment they were in. It was also dangerous because, more often than not, the IPSO, the officer who was in charge of the investigation units, used blatant manipulation and control. It was here that I realized the difference between giving information because you had a sense of loyalty to someone and giving information because someone was holding something over your head. Shane Halliday said, "The handler must be able to control the agent but not put himself above the agent." This was not the philosophy that an IPSO operated by.

To show you what I mean, let's go back to the reason I was in the hole. I liked to smoke hash at the end of each day after the cell door was locked for the night. It was a soothing escape from the monotony of prison life. The unfortunate part of smoking hash and pot when it came to drug testing was that it took up to forty-five days for these drugs to leave your system—in contrast to water-soluble drugs such as coke, meth, and heroin, which came out of your system in about seventy-two hours. For this reason, most inmates turned to the harder drugs to beat the random drug tests. I did not like the other drugs, and I paid dearly for not switching.

I was in the hole because I had failed the drug test for cannabis. The first time I failed, I spent fifteen days in the hole, and then I was let out. They let me out for a day and then tested me again. Since it had only been fifteen days, I failed again and received another fifteen days in the hole. The same process was repeated when I was let out the next time. The problem was that failing three tests in such a short period of time made me eligible for a transfer to a higher security prison.

I had been in the new prison less than a month when the IPSO and his partner drove the four hours to pay me a visit. The formalities lasted only seconds, and then they pulled out a recorder and offered me a deal. If I would tell them everything they needed to justify sending the top drug dealer at the prison I had just left to the one I was at now, they would wait a month or two and transfer me back to a lower security prison. I now knew why they had used the tactics they had on me. It was all a ploy to get the top drug dealer. It was unfortunate that they had not simply asked. I would have given them the information with a lot less trouble.

As I look back from my current perspective, I find it fascinating what went on inside the prison walls. It was unfortunate that there was so much hatred oozing out of both the guards and the inmates. The inmates demonstrated childlike behaviors, and the guards responded in predictable ways, demonstrating that they thought anger, manipulation, power trips, and excessive control were the best way to deal with temper tantrums. It seems to me that other guards could learn something from Don. They would be much further ahead if they used a little humility and genuine empathy to set an example for those in their charge. The manned gun towers and armed stations give the prison staff all the control they need to protect themselves and society. A little humility, where it can be applied safely, would go a long way to improve relations with those they are guarding.

Outside the Prison Walls

What do I want police handlers to glean from what I have discussed in this chapter? It is simple: Thinking that you are better than those you are handling will raise a red flag with any informant worth using. In my personal experience, any officer who raised that flag was a cop I could easily manipulate or a cop I would steer clear of. It is an attitude that will never bring good results in the long term.

Resilience

13

He that can't endure the bad will not live to see the good.

—Jewish proverb

I walked into the corner store to grab a chocolate bar and a bag of chips. As I stepped toward the cashier, a uniformed police officer did so at the same time. I offered to let him go first, but he politely declined with a smile. I watched as he put his coffee on the counter and took out his wallet. The cashier insisted that he did not have to pay and that the coffee was on the house. The officer looked at the lady and said, "Thank you very much. However, you have a business to run, and it would not be fair for me to take it for free." I was humbled just watching the interaction, although my sentimental feelings did not last long. As I was leaving, a lady stepped up to the counter and angrily demanded, "Do I get a free coffee too?" The response from the cashier was quick and to the point: "When you start protecting me, I will give you a coffee for free also."

The news always shows the wrong that police officers do, and, in a transparent society, I am happy when it is done factually and fairly after due process. What is unfortunate is that we do not often hear similar reports showing the issues that police face every day and the resilience they need to keep on working without hurting more people.

In my own experience, I have watched many arrests take place in which officers have taken punches during the takedown and not pressed charges. I have seen the opposite when a criminal was the one who got hurt during the takedown. I wonder how much taxpayers' money goes every year to criminals who start frivolous lawsuits for a punch they would not have received if they had surrendered when asked to. I'm not in any way condoning brutality. I am simply stating that takedowns are not always pretty and they can't always happen without a fight.

I have seen both police officers and prison guards get spit on, hit, kicked, and punched. I have seen cups of urine and human and animal feces thrown at them, and a myriad of other vile things done out of hatred toward those in uniform. I wonder sometimes what type of person it takes to endure this part of policing and how officers are able to rebound from it and move on to the next call.

Resilience is defined as "the power or ability to return to the original form, position, etc., after being bent, compressed, or stretched; elasticity." The fact that a majority of criminals sneak around in the dark of night should give a good indication that the job of a handler is going to require a great deal of resilience—especially if he has a family. Mike Cabana observed, "Anyone getting involved in this line of work needs to realize that information does not surface on a set schedule, Monday to Friday, 8:00 a.m. to 4:00 p.m."

On Call

In the early 1980s, when technology was not as advanced as it is today, it was not as easy to contact a handler when he was off shift. There were no cell phones, there were no emails, and no Skype, and the closest we could get to smartphones were the people who answered the phones at the detachments. If they were good at their job, they filtered the essential information from the nonessential and then made the decision to link or not link a source to his handler at home. Now, of course, in my mind, all the times that I wanted to reach Mike were essential—and in some ways that was true.

Mike Cabana observed, "Informants are people, and many of them bring significant baggage and regularly need assistance navigating through personal issues/events affecting them. A handler needs to be prepared to help to the extent possible."

Dramatic Intervention

I was traveling across the country to meet up with a girlfriend. I had not seen her in years but had been in constant contact with her on the telephone. This was not just any girlfriend but the very first love of my life, and I was really looking forward to seeing her again. With only about five hours of driving left before, I would reach the city where we intended to meet, I decided to stop for the night and have a few drinks.

It was a cold winter night in January, cold enough that in the five-minute walk from my hotel to the bar, ice had begun forming on my eyebrows and moustache. Not only had I decided to have a few drinks to while the night away, but I had decided to do it at a biker bar that I had never entered before. While biker bars in those days were my comfort zone, I was nowhere near my home town, where the bars were run by the Hells Angels. The bar I had picked to enter that night was run by their archenemies, The Outlaws. Not being very bright at the time, I was also wearing a shirt that said, "Support the big red machine," and had all the markings of a Hells Angels supporter. I will not relate here the story of how I made an ass of myself inside the bar and then barely made it out with my life; the details are in my previous book, *Treacherous*. The point of mentioning this story here is to illustrate the resilience of Mike Cabana.

Sometime between arriving at the bar and being chased out, I decided to call my girlfriend's mother. She gave me the awful news that Angie had died of a drug overdose. I was devastated and half drunk. It was around midnight, which, because of the time difference, made it somewhere between two and three in the morning where Mike was. I called the detachment and convinced an officer there to transfer my call through to Mike at home. I was drunk, distraught, dramatic, and not overly coherent. Amazingly, Mike stayed calm and talked to me for an hour, calming me down and convincing me to call him first thing in the morning when he was at the office. There was no hint of anger, irritation, or judgment in his voice. He was just a police officer putting on the hat of a psychologist at three in the morning and talking me down. It would be good if this was a one-time occurrence, but the truth is that this happened about once a week for years—and each time the call was just as dramatic and, in my mind, just as essential.

Hindsight is 20/20, and I can only imagine the affect this must have had on Mike's family. He had a wife who worked as hard as he did and young kids to take care of. The fact that I was such a constant disruption to the household makes me realize the level of resilience that Mike and his family must have had for them to endure that multitude of late night calls. My other handler, Shane Halliday, observed, "A handler must be available continuously during an operation and must be able to bounce back quickly even when any hiccups occur."

Innovative Thinking

The resilience it takes to handle the hatred and the scorn that sometimes come with being a police officer is fairly minor in contrast to the resilience it takes to do the job itself. Being able to rebound from a situation that did not go the way you expected or in a way that you trained for is essential to being a good police officer—and to the police officer's survival as well. When it comes to undercover work, especially dealing with informants, things going sideways is inevitable, which makes this characteristic even more important for handlers.

It is almost impossible to discuss resilience without bringing up the skill of innovative thinking. Whether in the course of everyday investigative duties or in the course of an undercover operation, these two skills go hand in hand. The ability to roll with the punches and think on one's feet is invaluable. Mike Cabana recalled one of the lessons he learned early on as a handler: "I quickly realized that the information being provided and/or the circumstances around the criminal activity the info related to seldom fit into a textbook case type of investigation. If something can go sideways, it inevitably will, and the handler needs to be prepared to figure out the best way forward."

Operation Joulable was the first time I had worked with an officer by my side on the streets, and it took some getting used to. At first, I was not convinced that the guy they had brought in could pass for a drug dealer; this is where I learned that sometimes the Mounties could see more from their vantage point than I could from mine. As it turned out, Dan and I got along great. He knew the game well and spoke the criminal language very proficiently. More importantly, he was able to think on his feet. He could respond to the most difficult of questions from a target without any hesitation. It was a skill I envied and one that got us through a few tight situations.

One time, we were at a suspect's house in the middle of nowhere. It seemed we were so far into the woods that we would have had to come out to hunt. The main suspect, a multipound drug dealer, may have been far out in the woods, but he was living in a beautiful house surrounded by forest and overlooking a river. This made it very difficult for a cover team to keep surveillance in a way that could help us if we got into trouble. Dan and I had just arrived and were having a beer while discussing a purchase of cocaine. Unexpectedly, there was a knock at the door. It was another major suspect, who would be very suspicious about why we were making a deal with his competitor, especially after we had just proposed an identical deal to him. Dan made up a quick story about why we could not be seen there, and the owner of the house hid us behind the bar while the two suspects talked. I remember looking at Dan, with a beer in his hand, ducked down behind the bar, both of us nervously smiling at one another as we listened. We had absolutely no idea if we were in danger or not, as the two drug dealers were speaking in French, a language both of us at that point wished we knew but didn't. In the end, the door closed, and we came out from behind the bar to have another beer.

The operation worked out, and both suspects were eventually charged. However, I often wonder how that situation would have turned out had Dan not been able to think quickly and calmly. Things could have taken a real turn for the worse had that skill not been there at the time we needed it. Paul Merton observed, "The thing about improvisation is that it's not about what you say. It's listening to what other people say. It's about what you hear."

Quick Thinking

In the last operation I ever did for the police, Operation Download, I came very close to being killed. Thankfully, because of the quick thinking of the officers involved and the actions of Shane Halliday, I am alive today, and the operation was a success. The following excerpt from my previous book *Treacherous* tells the story:

There were many times through the operation where there was a little suspicion on me. There were many times when I was patted down while wearing the wire and it was overlooked. There were a lot of times that I pushed the envelope by asking questions in order to pump for an incriminating comment on the wire. The two most dangerous people to push the envelope with were Neil Smith and Bobby Milton. Neil, being a Hells Angel, was very well disciplined to watch for suspicious behavior in everyone. And Bobby—well, Bobby was an old school biker, and though he was no longer an actual member of the Hells Angels, he had been a member almost from the start of the Halifax chapter. Bobby was the member who had mentored Neil in the beginning of Neil's journey as a probationary member. It was a dangerous thing to push the envelope with either one, but for me personally Bobby seemed to be the one to fear. Maybe this conclusion had come from living with him, maybe it was from being in prison with him, or maybe it was that his reputation had preceded him.

Bobby was volatile at the best of times. When I had been living with him, I would watch him wake up, drink half a bottle of methadone, eat a bowl of frosted flakes with White Russian instead of milk and then smoke crack all day—while still managing to do business like it was nothing. It was no wonder the scariest moment, and the one that brought the operation to an end, involved Bobby.

It started with a conversation that took place in March at the Corner Pocket, a private club run by the Hells Angels. Bobby was having a drink with me, and we were standing near the bar when some guy walked in. Bobby whispered in my ear something about the guy that I could not understand. He then went on to describe to me the murder of Mike Hamm back in 1985. He described how he had walked up behind Mike and shot him in the back of the head and how Mike's dog had whimpered and licked at the blood of his master while he was lying there dying. It seemed to be exciting Bobby as he told the story, and he started rocking back and forth. Whether Bobby was bragging, was testing me, or had actually done it is still a mystery. I do know this: Bobby's nickname was 'Rockin' Robert' because whenever he would participate in violence, he had a tendency to rock back and forth. The conversation did not end up on the wire because of a technical problem, but within a month the local newspaper had started a cold case series and had highlighted the Mike Hamm case twice, once on the front page.

If Bobby had not been suspicious of me before, he certainly was now. On Friday, April 13, 2001, Bobby called me and asked me if I had seen that day's paper. I was nervous but answered that I had. We discussed the article a little and then said we would touch base later and maybe meet at the Pocket. When the conversation was over, I commented that it had made me a bit nervous. I then headed to have a shower while Tina cooked supper. As I stepped out of the bathroom after my shower, Tina told me that Bobby was on his way over and asked me if she should make extra food. My stomach was instantly churning. I knew this was not likely going to be a good visit. I asked Tina for details of the conversation. She said that Bobby had called and said that he had found some teeth for me and that he was bringing them over to see if they fit. 'Teeth' is code for 'bullets.' I had been asking Bobby for bullets for my .38 for a while, I had seen him at least twice that day, and he had not mentioned them then even though he knew I really needed them. I quickly called Shane and asked him if he had been listening. He had. I told him to get us over to the safe house quick. Shane was there in minutes, and the police radios were humming. First, they set up surveillance on the apartment, and then they brought patrol cars into the area.

Tina and I listened to the excitement from the safe house on Shane's radio as information and directions were passed back and forth between the surveillance team and the others. Bobby arrived at the apartment, knocked on the door and of course got no answer. Then we heard the team say, 'He is looking in the window. Holy shit, he is going in.' Bobby went in and then called Neil from my home phone, which of course was tapped. He told Neil that I must have left in a hurry and then described the apartment to him. The decision was made to arrest him. In went the patrol car, and the police took Bobby into custody. Bobby later told an informant that his plan had been to take my gun under the guise of checking to see if the bullets fit my gun and then whacking me with my own piece.

Fortunately, we were safe. Shane took us to a hotel near the police station while the police figured out what to do. The decision came the next morning. They would hold Bobby for the long weekend and have me meet with Neil one more time on the following Tuesday. I was not crazy about this direction at all. It was obvious that Neil had been part of Bobby's plot, and now they wanted me to do one more meet with Neil. Were they crazy?

When this situation started to unfold, it did so very quickly. It was handled in a way that not only showed the ability of those involved to think on their feet but also highlighted their resilience. Within days, I did go back with their revised plan, and I was able to hammer the last nail into the coffin of a Hells Angel who had for years been able to avoid being convicted of any criminal offence.

Sense of Humor

14

A sense of humor is part of the art of leadership, of getting along with people, of getting things done.

—Dwight D. Eisenhower

If cultivating and handling informants is an art, then a sense of humor is one of the police officer artist's greatest tools, essential in the creation of any investigative masterpiece. Humor can defuse anger, calm fear, lift depression, relieve tension, build rapport, and create bonds. It is vital when dealing with a dark, sinister world. Many times, it is the only common ground for both those who are on the good side and those who are on the bad side.

I read an article not long ago about the benefits of humor in the workplace. The benefits the author of the article listed were similar to the ones I have just mentioned. However, the politically correct parameters he suggested for how humor should be used would never work in policing. For example, the author said, "Tasteful humor is the key to success at work." That is true for most of the businesses I have been involved with over the past fifteen years. However, in the clandestine world of cops and robbers, it is not realistic. There, neither the work nor the humor could be described as "tasteful."

A Macabre Tale

I recall one day sitting in a hotel room with a group of four police officers, waiting to go and testify in court. I listened as the officers conversed about some of the crazier experiences they had had dealing with death over their careers. One of the newer officers talked about a homeless guy who had been found not long before. It seems that the deceased had been lying there for some time, and when the police found him, his body was covered in maggots. There were so many larvae feasting on the remains that it looked as if the body was moving. This officer described the scene in detail and admitted that it had been too much for him and he had had to turn away to vomit.

Where was the humor in that? There was none. It was a horrifying sight for any human being to have to deal with. The humor came later, when the officer sat down for supper that night and his wife placed a big bowl of white rice on the table in front of him. The officer politely declined and pushed the bowl away, saying he was not very hungry. The officer laughed with his colleagues as he recalled that his poor wife must have thought he was saying there was something wrong with her cooking.

The dark humor in that story was followed up by other equally humorous stories, as the officers took turns talking about the suicides, murders, and other traumatic events they had experienced during their years on the force. Mahatma Gandhi observed, "If I had no sense of humor, I would long ago have committed suicide." Police humor may seem morbid from the outside looking in, but officers who do not learn to find humor in the horrible things they see often end up as suicide victims as well. They may be smiling when they tell these macabre stories, but there is sadness and pain in their eyes.

A Fish Story

There were a number of shifts in which the officers came to the hotel with a strong smell of fish and fuel on them. Evidently, the pilots of a cargo plane had miscalculated the weight of their load. Unable to get off the ground, the overloaded plane had crashed into a barrier at the end of the runway. I listened as the officers talked very somberly about the body parts they had recovered and the evidence they had tagged. Suddenly, one of the officers piped up and asked if anyone had tagged the skunk that had been found a couple of hundred feet in front of where the plane had come to a final stop. They all laughed as they discussed how the animal had probably had a heart attack when it had seen the monstrous metal object thundering toward it.

A police officer's sense of humor is used to relieve the stress of dealing with horrific sights that no one should ever have to see. Police humor may seem dark, politically incorrect, and even vile. That is why I have related only two very mild examples of police humor. However, no matter how others see it, a sense of humor is a vital ingredient in the making of a good cop. It is what gives police officers the ability to deal with inhumanity and still remain human.

Inhumane World

I walked into a small apartment where ex-Hells Angel Bobby Milton was hiding out down by the waterfront. I gave Bobby a quick hug and then went straight to the window to make sure I had not been followed. We had started a war with the black community, it was a territory the bikers did not want to give up, and now we had both groups wanting to take us out. There was light, powdery snow on the ground, showing only our footsteps coming into the building. We took out our guns and put them on the table while Bobby made us each a drink—his favorite, White Russians. We left our body armor on and took turns watching the only entrance to the dead-end street through a small window in the bathroom. It was a tense situation that could erupt into gunplay at any moment, just as it had twice before in the previous week. While one of us kept guard, with the door barricaded, the others in the apartment played cards, weighed and packaged cocaine for distribution, and listened to Bobby tell stories from the past.

As he told one story that night, Bobby could not stop laughing all the way through. It concerned something that had happened back in his money-collecting days. Apparently, he and his old partner had gone to collect some money from a small-time shoplifter who owed a drug debt. After following him to the mall, they waited for him to exit, came up behind him, threw a dog chain around his neck, dragged him to their car and threw him into the trunk. When Bobby and his twisted partner got their victim back to the hideout they were using, they began to torture him. It was at this point in the story that Bobby began to find humor. They beat the guy, urinated on him, and did a number of other unspeakable and degrading things to him. Then they decided to break the man's arm—but they couldn't do it. One of them laid him out on the floor and sat on him while keeping the arm outstretched. They began pounding on it with a metal bar, but it wouldn't break in the way they had hoped. (They couldn't understand it because it had always worked in the movies.) Finally, the two geniuses realized they needed a little more leverage for the type of break they desired. They placed the arm on two phone books, and with one swift crack they were done. They dropped their victim off near the mall where they had abducted him, throwing him out onto the pavement. Bobby laughed again as he recalled telling the guy he had a week to come up with the five hundred dollars that was owed or there would be another night of fun.

Why do I feel it was necessary to share this bit of dark humor from the criminal world? Two reasons.

First, in the bubble-wrapped society most people live in, it is hard to comprehend what goes on in that other society, the criminal world. By giving a glimpse into that evil world, I hope to show why I believe we need to cut those who protect us a little bit of slack and not demand that they be politically correct all the time.

Second, the humor needed to cultivate and maintain an informant is not going to come from a book of jokes. It's not going to come from the humor that's used at the supper table in a family home. It certainly is not going to come from the jokes told from a church pulpit. It is going to come from the improvised wit that is bred out of experience on streets of blood.

A Vital Skill

Shane Halliday, one of my handlers, observed, "You have to have a sense of humor and be able to laugh at your own mistakes." A sure sign for me that a police officer is going to be someone I can work with is that he is able to admit his mistakes and laugh at himself.

Now, do not misunderstand what I was saying previously to mean that I condone humor that is mean-spirited. Do not think that I believe that all police officers have a morbid or sick sense of humor. What I am saying, though, is that when we send frontline soldiers out to deal with the most horrendous of situations, let us put their sense of humor into the context of their environment. Let us not be quick to judge their humor by the same standard we would use for a joke told at a family picnic.

Why could I not work with someone who did not have a sense of humor? It should be obvious from what I have already said: "Humor can defuse anger, calm fear, lift depression, relieve tension, build rapport, and create bonds. It is vital for dealing with a dark, sinister world. Many times, it is the only common ground for both those who are on the good side and those who are on the bad side."

Going into the violent atmosphere of the criminal underworld is scary enough at the best of times. Going into the criminal underworld with the intention of disrupting its flow of income and putting its members in prison

Shane undercover in 1985 working a file involving the importation of opium

Shane undercover in 1984. Taking on the 13th Tribe MC
before they became Hells Angels

is even more nerve-wracking. Every moment could be your last, every friend could be your killer, and every situation is serious and volatile. If I can escape for a few minutes from the organized chaos of that hell in order to call or meet with my handler, I want to hear something funny. I expect my handler to have the ability to offer some witty remarks to help me unwind before I get down to the business of sharing the intelligence I have gathered.

The humor works both ways. I am sure that, as stressful as the work was for me, it was just as stressful for my handlers. They not only had to go into the underworld to take criminals down, but, in order to do so, they had to deal with the likes of me. The first part of this book shows a little of what that must have been like for them.

I am good at laughing at myself, and I have become fairly good over the years at recognizing my own mistakes. I know I can be witty, and I tried to use that when I saw tension in any officer I was dealing with, especially the ones who had to handle me.

I once told Mike that I was surprised that he had not lost his mind while dealing with me. His response was quick: "What makes you think I didn't lose my mind? Some would surely say that I did. I'm still dealing with you."

Discernment

15

To pursue a man effectively, it is best to begin with his thinking.

—**Louis L'Amour**
Last of the Breed

The dictionary defines discernment as the "ability to perceive by sight or some other sense or by the intellect; to see, recognize, or apprehend." In the world that I have been discussing, it is the ability that determines whether you will live or die. It is the one gift that police and informants have in common and the one they both depend on for survival.

If I look back over the murders that took place in the circles I traveled in over the years, especially the ones within organized crime groups, most of them have one common denominator. It is the hug and embrace before the bullet, the last meal and cheery laughter before the splatter of blood, the "Thanks for a second chance" just before the floor is covered in brain matter. Gary Ponzo depicted this very well in his novel, *A Touch of Deceit*:

'Thomas,' the boss said. 'How's your father doing?' 'He's good, Sal.' Always the family questions first. That was Sal Demenci's style. He could be about to whack someone and he'd ask how the guy's sister was doing in school.

Nervous Waiting

We crossed town in Shane Halliday's police-issued Chevy Blazer, heading across the bridge toward the Hells Angels stash house. I could tell that Shane was not crazy about making the stop and that he was sensing there could be trouble. As we neared the neighborhood, he crawled along until he found a vantage point high enough to oversee what we were doing. As he dropped us off, he made it abundantly clear that Tina and I had fifteen minutes to get in and get out and then make our way back to the truck, not one minute more.

We hurried down the snow-covered alleys until we reached the apartment. We rang the buzzer and stepped back from the door a bit so whoever was watching from the apartment would see that it was us. The door buzzed open, and in we went. When we reached the third floor, the apartment door opened just as I was about to knock. There was Bobby with his arms out and a big hug for me—partially out of love and partially to pat me down.

He wrapped his arms around me, patting me on the back and sliding his hands swiftly over any place where I might have stashed a weapon.

I had to stop Bobby as he tried to put drinks into our hands at the kitchen table. This, of course, made him a little suspicious. After all, it was Saturday morning about 9:30. Why would we be refusing a drink at the beginning of a busy work day? We were running out of time, so I quickly told Bobby that something had come up, we were going out of town to make some money, and we should be back in three weeks at the most. Any suspicions Bobby might have had were blinded by his greed. He knew that any time we went out of town to make money, it was never a small amount. The discussion quickly turned to how long I would be gone, what was expected of him and—most importantly—how much cocaine I would be leaving behind for the house while I was gone.

We were approaching the crucial fifteen-minute mark, and Shane was probably getting a little nervous waiting in the truck. I would not have been surprised if he was getting a little irritated as well. We were already putting up resistance to the plan to take us out of town to a hotel for three weeks to get any drugs we had out of our system before the operation started. On top of that, we were insisting that it would be suspicious if we just left town and did not stop and make an appearance at the stash house first. The police suggested we just make a phone call and say the same things we were planning to say in person, but we would have no part of that. So, here we were, angry, on our turf and apparently happy to leave Shane waiting outside by himself.

I told Bobby we had to get going as the snow was supposed to fall soon and the roads were going to get bad. I told him not to worry about the cocaine, that he could keep it all there and that it should last him until I got back to town. I did ask him to give me an ounce just in case I needed it along the way. He was ecstatic and more convinced that I would be back since I was leaving so much behind.

After a quick hug goodbye and then some ducking and weaving through the alleys, we were back at the truck. As we pulled away from the area, Shane looked at me and said in a serious tone, "I hope you got all that you came for today." I just let that go in one ear and out the other. Then I said, "This is the start of a long road, isn't it, Shane?"

A Gut Feeling

Shane Halliday has said, "Handlers need to know what is truly important in any operation. They must also have the wisdom and good judgment to figure out what is *really* happening in every situation." Had Shane known that I was stopping at the stash house to get drugs? After all, it was my drug house. Whether I was stopping to get drugs or stopping to give drugs, I am sure he had to be aware that I was likely up to no good. I have never asked him about this, but I think the reason he took the high vantage point was to protect himself from any setup and still be able to intervene in case all hell broke loose at our end.

So, was it a gut feeling that made him do that? Was it maybe a sixth sense? Was it perhaps a form of intuition? This is something that police and criminologists have studied for a long time without coming to any definitive conclusions. It seems simple to me. What Shane had was an ability to discern, a gift strengthened by wisdom gained through life experience, coupled with training and study. If you look at who survives in the world of organized crime, whether on the good side or the bad, it is always the one who has been trained, who continues to study, and who has gained wisdom through many days and nights of testing on the hardened streets.

An Open Question

Terry Galloway wrote, "Deafness has left me acutely aware of both the duplicity that language is capable of and the many expressions the body cannot hide."

A young police officer was sitting on the side of a lonely stretch of deserted highway in New Brunswick when a gold-colored Porsche flew by him at a ridiculous rate of speed. The officer threw down his paperwork, flipped on his lights, and pulled out to start a pursuit. Moments later, the officer was standing at the side of the New York–licensed sports car, staring down at the fidgety twenty-four-year-old driver. After the usual questions, the officer told the driver to sit tight and headed back to his cruiser to fill out a speeding ticket.

What happened next was mind-numbing. The driver, who was apparently already nervous from a shooting he had allegedly been involved with in New York, got out of his car, reached back inside for a high-powered rifle, and walked over to where the unsuspecting officer was writing up a standard speeding ticket. Without a second thought, the driver of the Porsche instantly killed thirty-one-year-old Constable Emmanuel (Manny) Joseph Aucoin. In one instant, two children were left without a father, a wife was left without a husband, and many other family members and friends were left asking why.

I only know this story through the news—and from the mouth of the killer, who was in a cell just down from me for about a year. I do not know anything from the investigation itself. I will say emphatically that there is nobody to blame for the death of Manny Aucoin except the killer who was convicted of his murder. Having said that, could discernment have done anything that morning to help even the odds and give this officer a better chance of surviving? Was there anything that could have been read at the scene that could have prevented the murder from happening? I do not know the whole story of what happened that day, and I do not have the answers. So, I will just ask the question: What made officer Aucoin comfortable or secure enough that he did not see this young man leave his car, get his gun, walk back to the cruiser, level his rifle, and shoot?

In the book *Don't Think of a Blue Ball*, Malti Bhojwani wrote, "I trust that when I am intuitive, it is a cocktail of all the information I have picked up along the way, which has come to me at the right time."

An Encounter with Wolves

Corporal Bourgeois and Constable O'Leary were two longtime police officers who had been working a kidnapping case involving the son of a prominent restaurant owner in their city. The boy had been kidnapped and then released after his father had paid a $15,000 ransom. The investigation had reached the point where the police were setting up roadblocks and searching cars in the hope of finding the suspects. A suspicious Cadillac was seen, and Bourgeois and O'Leary were asked to go after it and check it out.

There were only four people who knew the truth of what happened that day back in 1976, and only one of them is still alive. What we do know is that the police officers were overpowered at some point and likely thrown into the trunk of a car. We know that the two suspects handcuffed the officers to a tree about twenty to thirty feet from where two graves were dug. We also know that the suspects first tried to dig those graves with snow shovels but found that the ground was too hard. Receipts showed that they then drove into Moncton and bought shovels and picks at a hardware store at 8:15 a.m. on December 13.

We do not know all of the torture that these officers endured, although it likely included listening to the sound of their graves being dug. We do know that there was a scuffle at the tree where the officers were handcuffed and that O'Leary was shot in the shoulder. The two officers were then put into the graves and both shot in the head.

Christopher Shields has said, "There are three kinds of people in the world. There are wolves and there are sheep. And then there are those who protect the sheep from the wolves." If that is true, then who protects those who do the protecting? How did the bad guys get the jump on these two officers? As in the case of Manny Aucoin, what can we learn from incidents like this, and what role does discernment or an officer's sixth sense play in these situations where things have gone sideways?

Complacency and Alertness

It is my opinion that the enemy that drowns out most officers' ability to discern is complacency. Policing is one of those jobs that can become very mechanical and routine, even mundane, for long periods of time. Unfortunately, there is no room on the job for an officer to be daydreaming or thinking about the days ahead or what's for supper. Every officer has to be alive, alert, and aware each moment of the day, no matter how boring the job may seem to be at times.

Where were the alarm bells in these cases? Were they not ringing, or were they just not heard? When you know you are in danger, every fiber of your being should be studying, training, and learning. You should be on high alert, tuning into all that is going on around you, at least until you are out of the hunters' zone.

Witness Protection Coordinators 16

Witness protection has been universally recognized as one of the most important tools law enforcement has at its disposal to combat criminal activity.

—RCMP website

I find it fitting that this chapter is near the end of this part of the book. Why is that? Witness protection programs are one of the few ways to bring a gangster's life to a close. Many die in some forms of violent death, whether the weapon of choice is a forced drug overdose, a hail of bullets, a knife to the chest, or a pipe to the head. Worse yet, any one of these violent methods of committing murder is often employed after a long bout of torture. Some of the more fortunate criminals are able to live out their days in prison cells, still at risk of a violent demise; some might actually want such a death—anything to put an end to their unendurable existence. There are only very small groups who make it out of the crime world on their own. However, over the past two decades, there have been an increasing number of criminals who have escaped the criminal world by choosing "the program."

Over the past fifteen years, membership has been steadily rising in this fairly exclusive group of turncoats. This is a world I have come to know very intimately yet can only write about superficially. I am bound by acts of parliament and confidentiality agreements, so I must tread lightly. However, I am going to share what I can for the purpose of shedding light on some of the important characteristics of the handlers who keep watch over those in the program. Those who accept this job often refer to themselves as witness protection coordinators. I will not get into an argument over terminology, but I will agree that the job of handling "protected persons" has a much broader responsibility than the job of other handlers.

The documentary television series *Outlaw Bikers* had an episode called "Contract from Hell," about an elaborate sting operation that brought down some prominent members of the Hells Angels. At the end of the program, two adults watched as their two children were skipping to a waiting police car. I guess it was an attempt to depict them going off into the sunset under the umbrella of witness protection, a place where they would live happily ever after. It was an interesting take on entering the program, quite different from what is usually depicted in TV shows and movies. The usual scenario has armored vehicles, men in black, women in camouflage, and machine guns everywhere. Depending on the TV show or movie, there might even be a helicopter, with some bad guys trying to chase the team down as the family is whisked away.

That scenario was not my experience. When I entered the program, I did not skip off into the sunset, and the authorities did not need an army to get me out of danger. What they did use were specially trained men and women who, for the most part, took their job very seriously. Over the past fourteen years, I have dealt with witness protection coordinators with many different personalities, and I can say that all but two or three were a perfect fit for the job.

At the risk of some redundancy, I am going to speak about a few key characteristics that I believe are vital to being a good witness protection coordinator. I think it is important to emphasize the specific strengths needed for this position. Like the rest of the book, what I am presenting here are just my thoughts trickling out of my experiences and filtered through my biases. However, I believe that these thoughts have more validity than the thoughts of those who study the subject only in theory or from a safe distance.

Professional

Al Franken wrote, "Mistakes are a part of being human. Appreciate your mistakes for what they are: precious life lessons that can only be learned the hard way. Unless it's a fatal mistake, which, at least, others can learn from."

The first coordinator I had to deal with after entering the program was the one who I believed had ruined my life, putting me in a position where my only options were spending the rest of my life in prison or entering a witness protection. He is retired at this point, and I have already named him in my previous book, *Treacherous*. Therefore, in this case only, I will use a coordinator's real name. Al, in my opinion, made a bad decision that set off a tragic series of events. That decision not only brought my work as an informant to an end but also allowed a murder to take place that could and should have been prevented. It was a mistake in judgment on his part, one which caused me to file a lawsuit against the RCMP. It also gave me the motivation to write my first book, which was based on internal documents used in the civil proceedings.

I bring this issue up again in these pages, but not in order to affix blame or open old wounds. In fact, from my perspective at this point in my life, I believe both sides had valid points, and many positive changes resulted from the entire ordeal—although that may be a very little comfort to the murdered man's family. Hopefully, the good that came out of this incident will mean that his death was not completely in vain.

So, why do I bring it up? Al was my main handler for the first of my many years in the program. During that time, I was filled with hatred toward him for what I believed had been absolute negligence on his part. Not only was I suing the force during this time, but I was also submitting complaint form after complaint form in relation to his original actions. I did not stop there, though. With every decision he made while he was in charge of my protection, I filed more complaints and criticized both him and the RCMP in the media. I was such a pain in the neck that if I were in his shoes, I would have called the Hells Angels and given them my location, just to put an end to the accusations once and for all. That is why I bring this up. Not only did he not do any such thing, but if I am being honest, I would have to say that he was more professional in his work than even most handlers.

In a witness protection, you get to spend a lot of time traveling with your coordinators, many hours in which you can speak your mind and they can speak theirs. In the hundreds and hundreds of hours that I spent in conversations with these people over the years, I would have to say that Al was one of the more interesting. With our differences aside, I believe Al was one of those who were truly cut out for the job. I was treated with absolute professionalism, and he never let his emotions take over at any time. To me, that is quite extraordinary and speaks to both his training and his character. I am still absolutely convinced that he made a wrong decision that helped ruin my life, while Al and the RCMP are equally convinced that the fault was with me and not with any of them. Regardless of which side is right, the fact of the matter is that this dispute did not prevent Al from giving me respect, dignity, and the same level of protection that anyone else would have received. That is why I bring this matter up: even with the animosity between us, this member of an elite group of men and women remained professional.

Moral Compass

I have one more note regarding Al. At the beginning of this book, I stated adamantly that people should not be police officers if they do not have a strong moral compass outside of themselves. Al was a convinced atheist, and I had just made a commitment to being a Christian at the time we met. As a result, there was no shortage of issues to debate between us. I also said that if the Criminal Code was your compass, then it would be sufficient. In my eyes today, Al was a good cop who made a bad decision, but his moral compass, which seemed to be the Criminal Code, served him well throughout all his years as a policeman.

By the Book

According to Richard Castle, "People change when you're not looking."

Let's fast-forward to the year 2014. At this point, I had been kicked out of the program for about four years. For the most part, this was due to security breaches I had caused by writing a book, doing a documentary, and risking my own safety. Unfortunately, one of the original defendants from 2004 won his appeal and the right to a new trial. This meant that those who were currently managing the witness protection program were obligated to transport me safely to and from court, as agreed upon in my original contracts.

As much as I did not want to deal with my past all over again, I had no choice. Once again, I was back in the world of those who manage this top secret program. My first thoughts were of hesitation and even fear. These thoughts were soon replaced by the excitement of seeing all of the police officers, prosecutors, and handlers I had known before—and even the defendant. But I was taken off guard by the sudden realization that ten to fourteen years had passed since I had seen many of those who had been involved in the original trials. Most had moved on to new positions, some had retired, and a few had even died. I was also struck by the number of fresh, new faces. Many were as young as my children and had grown up in a much different time period than the one I understood. It was strange to say the least.

In 2014, it had been over thirty years since I had first been used as an informant. Most of the handlers I was now dealing with had less than half of that time in policing, and many had been in preschool when the first contract had been issued on my life by organized crime groups. In the meantime, money for police training had been cut back, rules had changed, and accountability was the new catchphrase. The covert world was now changing—for both good and bad. It was not the same environment that I had once known. Many may argue with me, but it is my opinion that the extreme amount of attention given to oversight has changed the focus of law enforcement. The focus is now on covering asses and saving money rather than on catching criminals and protecting informants, agents, and even the public. Accountability is always good, but in covert policing the oversight also needs to be covert. There are still a few old school guys around from the era when training was more intense and the mentality was different, but they are rapidly becoming extinct.

One of the old school coordinators, who I will call "Ron," was my main contact for the majority of my years in the program. If I said we butted heads on occasion, that would be an understatement, if not an out-and-out lie. Ron was Mr. RCMP, and everything he did was by the book. His note taking and his ability to remain silent drove me crazy. His assertiveness made me angry, and my inability to manipulate him made me want to lose my mind. It was

Ron who made the statement I quoted at the beginning of this book to the effect that I was the most manipulative bastard he had met in his career. I fought more with him than I did with almost any other police officer in my life. If you had asked me six or seven years ago, I would not have had much good to say about him.

Why is it that I did not like Ron? The long and short of it is that he was a good, strong handler and a very professional police officer. I disliked him because I could not manipulate him and I could not influence his decisions in any way. He held me accountable for all of my inappropriate actions (and there were many), regardless of the consequences and no matter how much grief that might cause him. Ron always played by the rulebook.

In 2013, I was lucky enough to have dinner with Ron during preparations for the upcoming trial. Earlier that year and in the years since I had left the program, Ron had made a point of texting to say "Happy birthday" to my children. After having dinner that afternoon, I was happy that I had had the opportunity to talk to him outside of the official role he had once played in my life. Why? Because I was able to see the difference between Ron the person and Ron the police officer who had a job to do and did it to the best of his ability. I was able to look back and remember things I might not have noticed before—the times he sent greetings on my children's birthdays, the way his reports were always truthful even if they showed either him or me in a bad light, and the times he showed he genuinely cared.

Intelligence and the Wisdom of Experience

Lyman Bryson wrote, "The error of youth is to believe that intelligence is a substitute for experience, while the error of age is to believe experience is a substitute for intelligence." As the quote implies, intelligence and experience are both necessary—and that is especially true of those who work in the witness protection program. Intelligence and wisdom must work together to produce a good coordinator.

I said earlier that I have met only a few handlers who were not fit for the job of coordinating those in need of protection. It is my opinion that if an officer has not had a serious amount of experience in policing or—even better—in the world of organized crime, then that officer should not be considered for this work. The person I will call "Chris" is a case in point. He seemed to have very little experience and, by his own admission, no real moral compass. This was very evident in his work.

As a person, I really liked Chris, and any time I had to travel with him I looked forward to whatever debates or discussions we were inevitably going to have. Very clearly, my issue with Ron was not a personality conflict; it was strictly with his ability to do the job. I would love to give examples of the many times his incompetence risked lives, but doing so would divulge witness protection procedures that should best remain secret. I will just say that there were many such incidents and that the root of the problems, from my perspective, was the lack of understanding of the seriousness of the job and the lack of a clear moral compass. Because he had no convictions of his own, he exhibited people-pleasing behavior and an absolute inability to think on his feet.

Only the Best

Witness protection is something that people enter very reluctantly for the most part. When people choose to take this route, it is usually at a time when they are afraid, desperate, and very vulnerable. At the same time, they are usually the type of people I described at the beginning of this book that are manipulative, greedy, and dangerous. It is for this reason that the officers picked to deal with those entering the program must come from the strongest of handlers. These specially chosen officers need to be able to control the manipulation, watch for danger, and help integrate an antisocial individual into a prosocial world. They must be able to alleviate fears, take away the sense of desperation, and create structure for each individual in their caseload.

There are many witness protection programs around the world, and as stated on the RCMP website, these programs are a vital tool in the fight against organized crime groups. Those who work in these programs are the wall that stands between the hunters and the hunted. It is for this reason that we must insist that they be the absolute best people we can find. If incompetence allows a predator to get through that wall, it will become harder to convince other potential witnesses to come forward and risk their lives to take down those at the top of the criminal underworld.

Partners in Crime 17

If you want to make peace with your enemy, you have to work with your enemy. Then he becomes your partner.

—**Nelson Mandela**

Human partnerships are something I have always found interesting to observe. It does not matter if it is a marriage, a friendship, a business relationship, or a partnership in the crime world. In the latter context, partners can be joined together in order to commit crimes or to solve them.

I will begin with partnerships formed to commit crimes. If you accept the idea that "birds of a feather flock together," then you would think that my partners would be sneaky and untrustworthy. The fact is that most of those I hooked up with were loyal to a fault. Three friends, in particular, come to mind. These three were devoted both to crime and to me, devoted in a way that most people could not fathom. When they said they were my partners, they meant forever in everything.

Brent

Brent was a bank robber and a self-admitted hit man. He was a gangster through and through, and it was obvious that he had been mentored by some hard-core criminals. With his brother and some other associates, he spent years going across the country practicing his art in all sorts of crazy, daring, and dangerous escapades. There is nowhere he would not go and not much he would not do to make a big score or help out an associate.

I worked my way up into Brent's world with two quick moves. First, I became friends with a former enforcer for The Outlaws motorcycle gang who now sold heroin for Brent. Second, I stuck like glue to this enforcer until my talents were noticed and required. This process was neither long nor difficult.

Brian had once robbed banks with Brent until one day when they were both involved in a spectacular police chase. This chase ended with them in handcuffs, and they spent the following years in one of Canada's most dangerous prisons. It was while in prison that Brian's life took a turn that it would be hard for him to ever recover from—he became addicted to heroin. It was fortunate for me that when I met Brian, he could not make money if he was standing in it—a common failing throughout the criminal world. Using his own product not only stopped Brian from prospering financially but eventually killed him.

How did I use Brian to climb upward? By the same method I used throughout most of my career: I would take failing drug enterprises and either make them prosperous or give them the appearance of success. I did this by using the money I received from the police or the money I acquired through being a fraud artist. In this case, as in many others, I shone as a real good earner.

Those at the top of the crime world are always on the lookout for money-makers. When they find them, they usually try to recruit them, in the same ways a pimp tries to recruit whores—either by enticing them with promises of grandeur or by intimidating them with violence. Brent was one of the few who did not use either of these tactics. Instead, he used his skills, his charisma, and his authenticity. He was exactly who he appeared to be a loyal gangster who would kill or die for those close to him.

Brent was the type of friend who tried hard to teach his associates everything he knew about being a criminal. I can remember him telling me that if I was ever being interrogated, I should pick a spot on the floor and stare at it. He taught me not to carry anything but a framing hammer and some screwdrivers—because they were tools, not weapons. I remember how he would go nuts when one of his drivers drove over the speed limit. It was always his belief that if you wanted to be a successful criminal, you should blend in, drive a family car, obey the laws of the road, and not bring unnecessary heat on yourself.

Brent died not long after a bad drug deal. He mysteriously went off the ninth floor of his apartment building when he was supposed to be on his way to my house with a load of cocaine.

Mikey

Mikey was not so secretive about his criminality, nor did he keep it a secret if you were someone he disliked. Most who knew him feared him—and rightfully so. He was so engrained in that world that everyone assumed that because he lived by the sword, he would die by it.

I had been out of prison for about two months and was sitting at the back of a strip joint run by the Hells Angels. It was dark, and the lights had just begun to move around, indicating that another girl was about to start grinding on stage. As I watched to see who was going to dance next, I glimpsed

Mikey come through the entrance to the bar area and stand as a towering presence by the door. I jumped up and walked quickly toward him. In seconds, we had hugged and were headed to a table away from the girls I had been sitting with so we could drink and talk. It was hard to believe Mikey was out of prison and was sitting in front of me. We made plans to hook up the next day and see what we could do together.

My good friend Mike McIntyre "Mikey" in Dorchester Penitentiary

The list of moneymaking ventures Mikey and I were involved with and the exploits that Mikey undertook would fill a book by themselves. I could talk about the time the Hells Angels threatened him and he went out looking for them, to hunt them down. I could relate how he fought back-to-back with another inmate in prison when they were attacked by a group with weapons. I could describe how he always walked into trouble to stick up for the underdog. However, the character of this partner can best be brought out by relating the last thing he ever said to me before driving his car head on into an oil truck, which killed him instantly. It was in a letter he sent me when I was about to get out of a halfway house in Ontario and he had just been released from prison after a parole violation. In a long, heartfelt message, he said that he was sorry he had not been there to watch my back and that he had missed me while we had both been incarcerated. He ended:

"Hang in there, brother. You have two hundred and sixty-five pounds of loyalty coming your way."

Steve

Brent was a mentor who would give his life for me. Mikey was a protector who would give his life for me. The third friend was Steve. Steve and I would not have considered each other partners, but we really were on many levels. Steve was a close friend and a follower. He would have been a top employee and a first-rate partner if it had not been for a serious drug addiction. In my first book *Treacherous*, I described how he killed for me and then traded his freedom for a prison cell, taking a life sentence rather than betraying anyone else involved in the crime.

In any partnership, there need to be certain qualities and clearly defined roles. There must be loyalty, trust, camaraderie, and many of the other qualities I have said that are the marks of a good handler. These qualities and a clear understanding of who will lead and who will follow are vital to any partnership alliance on the streets of blood—and in the police cars that drive on those streets.

Andy and Mike

I have described some of my experiences as a partner in the crime world. Now I will relate some observations I have had made watching partners in police circles.

Andy and Mike were two police officers that I liked from the first night I met them. They had completely different personalities but complemented each other perfectly. Andy, who was a former dog handler, was everything that the public should expect from a police officer. If my mother was to go to a police station, it is an Andy that I would want her to meet. I could be sure that he would be polite, helpful, detailed, dressed very conservatively, and willing to bend over backward to make the experience as stress-free for her as possible. Andy went by the book, and you always knew what to expect.

Mike, also known as "Sally," was a whole different story. The best way to describe him is to say that he acted as if he had come out of a Mel Gibson movie such as *Lethal Weapon*. I first met Mike officially after a murder investigation, but previous to that I had seen him many times in the bar I frequented when he had been doing surveillance on me. I would not have pegged him for a police officer. Sally was the kind of guy most criminals would have gladly given information to—because he seemed so unlikely to be a police officer. He was unshaven, dressed in jeans and a T-shirt, and was willing to do whatever it took to get the bad guys, regardless of how it would affect his career.

The loyalty and professionalism between Andy and Mike were unmistakable. However, what was outstanding in this partnership was the combining of diverse talents. Maybe that is something that is always attempted when senior officers decide who goes where, but based on my observations, it sure does not always seem like it.

Chris and David

Next, I want to look at two sets of partners from my witness protection days, coordinators who were in a very risky situation trying to protect those who were being hunted.

Chris was the coordinator I said should never have been given the job. That was not true of his partner. I think an attempt was made to join Chris with someone who had all the qualities needed to make up for all the things Chris was lacking. It was a guy named David who was given the job. I still pray for him today. I cannot imagine being stuck with a partner you have to carry all the time. I watched as David tried hard to justify behaviors that were just insane, given the job that they were supposed to be doing. What stood out the most to me, though, was not Chris's lack of abilities, which David had to compensate for, but Chris's lack of loyalty. Every time Chris had an ear that would listen, he would complain about the force and gossip about the other members. I soon realized that if he would talk to me that much to express his discontent with others, then it was likely that he would be saying the same kinds of things to others about me.

Ultimate Partners

The final people I want to talk about are the last set of partners I encountered before I left the witness protection program. They could not have been more compatible or more perfect for their job. If those in charge are looking for a model of the perfect partners, they need look no further than these two. They demonstrated respect for one another, compassion, loyalty, and every other positive quality I have spoken about so far. Their roles were clear, and they played by the rules in everything they did. I stayed loyal to the RCMP for a lot of years, and it was mainly because there was uniformity straight across the country. The officers were all trained the same way, in contrast to municipal forces, which varied greatly. With the RCMP, I knew I was likely to always be dealing with the same playbook. This last set of partners reminded me of the days when RCMP training was uniform all across the country; sadly, that is no longer the case.

This chapter reminds me of just how much of policing is relational. It's no wonder the divorce rate is so high in this world. What a balancing act it must be to try to be a partner at home while trying to remain a partner in crime.

Why did I write this chapter? Originally, I wanted to compare the partnerships in the police world with partnerships in the crime world, showcasing the types of partners who excel on each side. These partnerships epitomize many of the positive qualities I have discussed throughout this book: loyalty, rapport, a willingness to face danger and death, and discernment. This chapter embodies the central theme of this book, the partnerships between police officers and their informants. However, if I am being honest, my motivation goes back to what I said at the beginning of this chapter: I simply enjoy observing relationships, especially relationships in the crime world.

Looking Back

Blank Stares

Blank stares of the living dead,
Not much heard and not much said,
So much pain behind their eyes,
Existing as a lonely heart cries.

Cop or con, these words are true:
Death and destruction will harden you.
The world you share is the very same.
Know this now: it is no game.

If you enter in, please be aware
You are all in danger of getting that stare.
Gangsters, I warn you it does not end well.
Officers, please hear me:
The demons you fight are straight from hell

—Paul Derry

Looking Back

Gifts and Curses of an Informant

18

I was blessed with a gift. It's a gift and a curse. It never ends.

—Dan Fogelberg

The music of Black Sabbath was blaring in the rental car as I drove across the country. The song "War Pigs" drowned out every noise around me while I was lost in my own little world. The thought that I was paying so much attention to the music that I barely focused on the road is a scary one, to say the least; however, it gets worse. I drove for at least half a mile with a police car on my tail, its lights flashing and its siren wailing, and I was oblivious to its presence the whole time.

Needless to say, when the officer approached the car, he was not in a very happy or pleasant mood. In fact, I would have to say that he was pissed off to the max. It is kind of ironic that I was pulled over five hours from where I had rented the car but within sight of the detachment in which Mike Cabana had just recently started working. It must have been a coincidence because my destination was still sixteen hours away—but it was just the break I needed.

Why do I say it was a break? Informants—at least, those who are good at it and survive for any length of time—have many gifts. Unfortunately for our handlers—and lots of times for ourselves—these gifts can also become our biggest curses. In this case, it was my gift of being able to drop names quickly that worked to my benefit. I don't mean the type of name-dropping people do when they want to brag about the important people they know so that they, too, sound important. I mean the kind of name-dropping that opens doors—or, in this case, calms down a very irate police officer who did not know that I was in the process of stealing the rental car I was driving.

The ability to insert a name carefully into a conversation is a great gift when it is done correctly. I have worked my way into chapters of the Hells Angels on at least two occasions just by knowing when to let a name slip. However, when this is done incorrectly, especially in the crime world, it can get you hurt pretty quickly.

In this case, I handled the irate police officer by giving a sincere-sounding apology and then offering an excuse. I explained that I was lost and had been focused on trying to remember the directions I had been given to get to the local RCMP detachment. I watched as his eyes locked on mine and he quickly asked what reason I had for going to the station. "To see my good friend, Mike Cabana," I replied casually, and then I watched as his whole demeanor changed. After a quick trip back to his car with my identification in hand, he returned with a ticket for speeding and sent me on my way. Of course, I now had to drive to the detachment and ask for Mike, just to be safe. Thankfully, he was not around, and I was able to get right back onto the highway.

I will say that on this occasion name-dropping was a gift. With the Hells Angels, it was also sometimes a gift. However, on many other occasions, it was a curse and not a gift of any kind. On one of those occasions, it involved another biker gang, and it almost got me killed.

Curse

I had been sitting at a strip bar affectionately known as "The Zoo" for about three nights in a row, after a girl I was seeing started dancing there. I would alternate between the bar and a pool hall on the other side of town; in both places, I would sell cocaine while waiting for her to finish her shift. On this particular night, it was near the end of her shift, and I was just waiting for her to finish so we could get home and count the money we had made that day.

I got up to go into the men's washroom and was followed in by two big guys who looked like bikers. I was fairly new to this area and at that time had not dealt with any clubs that were not associated with the Hells Angels. The two bikers waited until I had finished and was turning to go out. Then they stopped me and asked who I was bringing girls to the club for and who was supplying my cocaine. They obviously were looking to muscle me in case I was planning on making lots of money in their club. At that point, I made one of the dumbest mistakes of my career by insinuating that I was associated with the Hells Angels and it was their dope. I thought that by saying this, I would be guaranteeing myself a safe passage out. Instead, the one guy showed me the club colors tattooed on his arm. It was the same arm he began hitting me with. The colors belonged to The Outlaws, a rival club to the Hells Angels.

I learned my lesson in name-dropping in the crime world that night. That lesson costs me a beating, a loss of pride in front of my woman, and the loss of all the money and drugs I had on me that day—not to mention the fact that I was not able to go back into that club again.

Mike Cabana not looking very impressed

Gift of Gab

My next biggest gift and worst curse was my ability to talk, a gift obviously related to my ability to drop names. As an informant, if you cannot tell a good story or dazzle people with words, you are not likely to ever get anybody to give you information. Gaining information usually requires an ability to talk but also a willingness to wear your sins on your sleeve, so to speak. If you want others to give you information about their dirty deeds, it usually means you have to share your dirt first.

This gift of gab actually works great with criminals but not so well with police officers. If I was to go back and try to remember all the times I have caused my handlers grief with my big mouth, it would be a nearly impossible task. Over the years, I have asked Mike Cabana, Shane Halliday, and my longest-serving witness protection coordinator how they ever put up with some of the things I have said that either offended or caused security issues. They are as puzzled as I am that they did not just shoot me.

Women

Besides name-dropping and having a big mouth, my next biggest gift— and my next biggest curse—was my ability to attract women. I found that women could be a big asset in my line of work. It was always easier to gather information with a good-looking partner on my arm to distract and disarm the target. Even in the criminal world, there were many men who would brag much more when a woman was around than if I had been by myself. This proved to be a great asset. However, from a police perspective, it could be a nightmare, especially when an informant has separated from, or even just gotten into a fight with, a spouse who knows he is a rat.

The mother of my oldest child was the first one to prove this theory true. Unfortunately, I do not learn quickly, so she was not the last. I don't remember how I ended up telling her that I was an informant, but I am guessing it was in a moment of intimacy when I was feeling very trusting. Regardless of when, the fact is that I not only told her that I was a rat but also told her that then Constable Mike Cabana was my handler.

It was not long after this that we got into a big fight. Straight to the courthouse she went; she was on a mission. The reason for her going to the courthouse was that I had not been home for a day or two but she knew I had a court appearance that day. I was fortunate and made it out of the building before she arrived. Sadly, Mike was there on another matter that day, and it was not long before he was on the receiving end of the wrath that was meant for me. The spectacle did not impress Mike, and it did not make his bosses happy either that I had told this woman about him. It was years before I left her completely, and in the meantime I did my best to do damage control. However, as William Congreve observed, "Hell hath no fury like a woman scorned."

To sum it up in layman's terms, informants like me use their name-dropping skills, their big mouths, their ability to attract women, and their skills at manipulation in order to get information. This can be a great benefit to their police handlers. But these same gifts can also create huge problems. When informants use their big mouths to brag to their women, it can endanger their handlers as well as themselves.

Taking a Life

19

Guilt is anger directed at ourselves—at what we did or did not do. Resentment is anger directed at others—at what they did or did not do.

—Peter McWilliams

As we drove away from the murder scene, I thought I was going to throw up. Just the words being spoken were enough to produce this response. This is surprising in one sense because I can barely remember hearing much of the conversation, at least not audibly. It's not that I can't remember the words. It's just that the picture the words were painting in my head as I heard them was so overpowering. The insanity and inhumanity of what had just happened was about to change a lot of lives forever.

I am going to share the description I gave of the murder in my first book *Treacherous* and then offer some thoughts regarding what I wrote:

In the car on the way over to Dartmouth to commit the murder, I was doing the driving. Wayne James was in the passenger seat, and Tina and Dino were in the back.

As we pulled up near the apartment complex, time seemed to slow down. A minute felt as though it was an hour, the quiet between heartbeats was deafening, and the shallow breathing of the four of us was all I could notice, even through the eerily calm conversation in the car. Who would shoot him? Which way would we run? Where would we meet after? This entire dialogue between the front and back seats was muffled by the questions going around in my own head. How could I stop this? Would they ask me to be the shooter? Were we going to get away from here alive? Were we really going to kill Sean for such a stupid reason? We were.

Inside the apartment, Sean Simmons, Steven Gareau, and others were doing crack cocaine together and drinking.

Gareau told the others he was going for beer, but instead he met our car just down the street at a muffler shop. Dino got out of the car and walked back to the apartment with Gareau. Steve rang the buzzer, and Sean came to the door to let him back in.

When Sean answered the door and saw his friends, he welcomed them in and reached out to hug them. It was Dino who had been chosen to do the shooting. Acting as if he were opening his arms to engage in the embrace, Dino pulled out the .32 revolver and shot Sean in the chest. Dino later said that fear gripped him at that point and his adrenaline began to pump. Mine would have too. After all, he had just shot a good friend. That was true even though Dino's friend happened to be an associate of the former president of the Hells Angels–and the sworn enemy of the acting president.

Sean was a big man, a boxer and a longshoreman; it took two more bullets to bring him down, another in the chest and one in the head. It then took him nine hours to die.

After Dino shot Sean, he came back to the car, and we took off out of there in a hurry. Steve Gareau ran out the back door of the apartment and went to a bar, where he called a cab and then went back to the hood.

I remember driving away from the scene feeling numb. We had just carried out a contract killing for a Hells Angel. It's not that I was surprised that Neil Smith had had Sean Simmons killed, but I was shocked that I had played such a huge part in it. After all, I had thought that I was one of the good guys.

I have argued with the RCMP, prosecutors, justice department lawyers, friends, and family as to whether I was a good guy or a bad guy when I was driving to the scene of the murder. I have fought the same fight in my own head and heart. The answer, if I am being honest, is a bit of both. I was playing a role—I have no doubt about that. I have never liked violence—I have no doubt about that either. There is also no doubt that I was one hundred percent convinced that Sean Simmons would not die during any operation I was involved in. Even in the car on the way to the murder, I was certain that somehow I could stop it. Where I do question myself and my motives is in whether my common sense was clouded by my own selfish desires. Did I want an operation so badly that I had allowed Sean to be left unprotected as bait? Or was I so cocky and prideful in my abilities as an informant that I had thought that the murder could never happen? Had I got so caught up in the role that I had not been able to come out of character? Did I really need the direction of the RCMP to keep me from going too far while acting as a gangster? I believe there is truth in each of these thoughts, but there is one overarching reality that cancels out all other questions, and that is that Sean is dead.

There is no question about where I was when Sean Simmons was shot. I was in the car waiting to help the killer make his escape.

Perspective

Commenting on this incident, Mike Cabana told me in an e-mail, "I also understand the decisions/interpretation made by others in relation to whether you were acting at the direction of the RCMP. I guess we are back to the issue of perspectives." What Mike was saying is that although he understood my view of the issue, he could also understand the position of the police officers involved. Mike knew that I was probably not going to like what he was saying to me, but he also knew that it was important for me to understand that all of the allegations and accusations just came down to a difference in perspective. That is one of the things that a good handler does—he helps put things into perspective for the informant.

This murder took place over fourteen years ago. They say time heals all wounds. I would have to disagree. I will say, though, that it can help to change our perspective. When I wrote about the murder in *Treacherous*, I was experiencing strong feelings of both resentment and guilt. At this point in my life, I feel only guilt for my own actions, both of omission and commission. The resentment toward others and their roles has faded. It has now been replaced with a desire to make a difference rather than lay blame.

What did I learn from the murder I took part in, and what can police glean from my thoughts and actions? Let's take some of the questions that were going around in my own head and see what we can learn all these years later:

1. Was common sense clouded by my own selfish desires?
2. Did I want an operation so badly that I had allowed Sean to be left unprotected as bait?
3. Was I so cocky and prideful in my abilities as an informant that I had thought that the murder could never happen?
4. Had I got so caught up in the role that I had not been able to come out of character?
5. Did I really need the direction of the RCMP to keep me from going too far while acting as a gangster?

Hindsight is 20/20. It offers a wonderful opportunity to see clearly the truths of the past, but only if we are open to those truths. As we look at the questions I posed in light of the first section of this book, then I think the answers become very obvious. I was selfish, I lived for operations, and my arrogance overwhelmed me, especially during the time around the murder. Therefore, the answer is an unequivocal yes to each of the first four questions. In fact, I think the fourth question could be stated even more strongly: Was I enjoying the criminal notoriety, fame, and lifestyle so much that I forgot that I was attempting to get an operation? The answer is yes. There is a saying that the road to hell is paved with good intentions. I could have had the best of intentions in wanting to keep Sean alive. However, I was so caught up in my own life that I did not want to see what should have been so obvious right in front of me.

This brings us to the last question. Did I really need the direction of the RCMP? Interestingly enough, I wish I had had the direction of those whom I had trusted in these situations for so many years. But in this instance I was not working under the direct supervision of anyone but myself. In my mind,

I believed then—and still do today—that I had an embedded sense of direction, an essential understanding of what I should do, based on my previous communications with police officers and my years of experience. However, I did not act on that sense of direction. Sean Simmons could have been saved if at any time I had just decided to take the information to another agency.

In the dark world of good guys and bad guys, there are logical connections between darkness and light, shipment and payment, and mistakes and consequences. When informants go undercover over and over again, it will have an impact on their understanding and their actions. Every once in a while, they need to be pulled out of the darkness so a proper assessment can be made of where their head is at. If this is not done, trouble will inevitably arise. Whether an informant is trying to get information on a murder, a drug enterprise, or a stolen bike, it is impossible for the informant to go snooping around in the dark without banging his head, gaining a new fear or two, encountering temptation, or losing perspective. Whatever the specifics are, there is no doubt that there will be issues that need to be dealt with. When you wander around in the dark too long, you can get lost.

This is where I believe the handler can be of great assistance. If handlers can take the time to be with their long-term informants, talking and listening and questioning and observing, it would be time well invested. A handler needs to communicate clearly and concisely the role and responsibility that an informant has—and the roles and responsibilities the informant does not have. This would go a long way toward keeping the informant on the straight and narrow path he should be following.

Prevention Is Better Than Regret

I no longer have the resentment I once had toward others in relation to the murder of Sean Simmons. I no longer look at what others could or should have done to make sure it did not happen. What I am left with is a lot of guilt that I will never overcome. As long as I walk this earth until my own death, there will be moments in time when I stop and stare off into the darkness. In that darkness, I see Sean's face and think about his children, his wife, his mother, and his sister.

Maybe through speaking and sharing these experiences, I can make a difference, so that someone else will not have to die in the future. It is my hope that, by picking my brain, police handlers will improve—and that therefore those they handle will also improve. It is my desire that this warning will impact the conduct of police officers and informants, so that they never have to live with the hell of knowing that they have contributed to the taking of a life.

Hours on the Stand

20

Truth, like gold, is to be obtained not by its growth, but by washing away from it all that is not gold.

—Leo Tolstoy

I stepped inside the front door of our house after saying goodbye to a friend who had just driven me home. I had commented to her that I felt as though I had suddenly contracted the flu. One minute I had been feeling fine, and the next minute I was sweating and nauseous. I felt cold as ice as I fumbled for the lights and put down the food that I had brought home with me from my restaurant. I turned up the heat and mumbled to myself that I felt as though I had just swallowed a softball. The house was lonely and dark. My girlfriend Tina was in the hospital, and the kids were with friends. I wandered around the kitchen trying to make a hot tea with lemon but finally gave up, went to the bedroom, and fell into bed.

When I woke up the next morning, I was drenched, literally lying in a pool of sweat. I was shaking, but I knew a friend from our church was coming to pick me up so I could go to visit Tina at the hospital. I pulled myself together and got showered, dressed, and ready to go; it seemed like an enormous task just to accomplish that much.

When my friend arrived to pick me up, I jumped into his truck and said good morning. He looked at me and asked me if I was sure I wanted to go since I was looking very pale. When we got to the hospital and walked into Tina's room, she took one look at me and told me to go down to emergency. I hated hospitals and refused, saying I just needed to go home and sleep it off. She was angry but told me that I was as white as a ghost and I should either get to emergency or go home to bed.

Forty minutes later, I was changing the drenched sheets and crawling back into bed. I passed out and slept until sometime early the next afternoon. This time, when I woke up, I was somewhat delirious. I reached for my .38 caliber handgun and started checking room by room, convinced that someone was there to kill me. It took me ten minutes to clear the house, but I could not shake the feeling that I was going to die, even after I knew the house was empty.

I was drained, completely emptied, and just fell back into bed, ready to surrender to anyone who could make this feeling go away. But the feeling

115

would only get worse. I woke up just before midnight, scared, and in awful pain. It felt as though someone was taking a brick and scraping it around the inside of my chest.

I went out to my truck and prayed it would start, as it had not been working well lately. Thankfully, on this night, it did. I drove to the hospital and presented myself to the emergency room. After taking one look at me and hearing my story, they strapped me to a bed, started giving me nitroglycerin, hooked up an IV, and called for a cardiologist. I remember that they kept asking me over and over again how bad the pain was on a scale of one to ten. I was beginning to wonder if they had heard what I had been saying about a brick scraping around the inside of my chest.

When all was said and done, the doctors chalked it up to a stress-induced heart attack. It could be that the new house, the new restaurant, and my whole new prosocial way of living had produced the stress that had brought it on. I doubt it. I am guessing that it had more to do with the fact that I was two weeks away from testifying as the Crown's star witness in a major Hells Angels murder trial.

After I had spent almost three weeks in the hospital, which had resulted in a one-week delay in the trial, I was on my way to the witness stand. Andre Gide wrote, "There are very few monsters who warrant the fear we have of them." It may be true that there are only a few monsters who warrant the fear we have of them, but three of them were about to stand and face their accuser—and that accuser was me. It's no wonder that I had had a heart attack.

I arrived in the city late at night and was taken to a meet spot, where my witness protection coordinators passed me off to the emergency response team (ERT). It was an intimidating process that insinuated danger at the very least.

Once I was safe at my location, with the door closed on my sleeping area, I literally felt my knees give out, and I fell into a nearby chair. One of the ERT guys stuck his head through the doorway to see if I was alright and then reminded me to be ready to leave early in the morning. I said, "No problem," and then made my way to the bed. I would like to say that I fell asleep quickly after a long day of stressed nerves, but that was not the case. I lay on that bed for hours just staring at the ceiling, wondering how it would all play out in court. What was it going to be like to see Wayne again? How many of my family would be there to support him or intimidate me? After all, he was married to my cousin, and it was causing a lot of tension to say the least. What would it be like to see Neil? Would there be a lot of supporters there for him? After all, he was a full patch member of the Hells Angels, one who made the club a lot of money. Then there was Dino, a ruthless street kid who loved everything about the gangster life. Most of all, he loved blood and causing pain. He was a born and bred killer and Wayne James's nephew.

I could not sleep at all, knowing that not far from me, somewhere in a cell, these three men were also lying in a bed and also likely having difficulty sleeping. They were not afraid of me because I was a violent person but because I held their secrets and they were about to enter the fight of their lives, desperate to keep anyone else from hearing them.

Betrayal

Someone has written, "Those who don't know the value of loyalty can never appreciate the cost of betrayal." If I said it seemed a little surreal the next morning when I was being whisked away to the courthouse, it would be a little bit of an understatement. If the vehicles themselves had not given the sense that this had to be a movie, then the guys in tactical gear surrounding me sure did.

Once safely at the courthouse, I was escorted past the holding cells, which some time in the next hour would be filled with the very monsters I had been so fearful of the night before. After a short elevator ride to the top floor, I was placed in a jury room, which would be my second home for a long time to come. The sound of radio checks and "all clears" would begin to grate on my nerves before long. In fact, as much as the situation was movie like, it was nowhere close to entertaining. It was nerve wracking yet tedious, adrenaline pumping yet tiring. All in all, it was a downright freaky experience.

Finally, it came, the moment I had been dreading for what seemed like forever. The sheriff opened the door and said, "Time to go." Two officers cleared the hallway in front of me; one went to the side entrance to the courtroom, while the other one, dressed in plainclothes, slipped through the front entrance and blended in with the crowd as a spectator. With two sheriffs in front of me and two more emergency response team members behind me, I walked as confidently as possible to the side entrance and into the courtroom. I was surprised my legs did not betray me as I walked past those whom I was about to betray.

Neil was closest to the door, standing next to his lawyer, Anne Derrick; then came Wayne and finally Dino with his lawyer. Neil stared into my eyes with a blank look, Wayne stared at me with a sad look, and Dino snarled, exactly as I had expected he would. I walked past the prosecutors and the court reporter to take my place on the witness stand. When I turned toward the packed courtroom, I sensed all the people in the room, including the jury members to my left, staring intently at me. In all my years as an informant, it was the first time I had ever testified—but it would not be the last. In fact, I have spent more time on the witness stand than I could ever have imagined I would, probably amounting to hundreds of hours. A decade later, in 2014, I was on the stand again to testify in an appeal regarding this case.

Collateral Damage

Testifying at the original trial was a sad experience to say the least. I said earlier that this murder changed a lot of lives forever. This was very evident in that courtroom. The grief of the family was strong, and I could see the jury's empathy for many of those involved etched in their faces each time I watched them enter or leave the courtroom.

I learned two very important pieces of information in all of the days I spent on the stand. The first is that there are so many faceless victims in a murder. The obvious ones are the victim's family, and the not so obvious ones are the defendant's family. However, the list is much longer than that. The victims include the first responders, all of the police officers who were involved throughout the investigation, the nurses and doctors at the hospital, and the technical workers whose job it was to clean up the blood and brain matter after everyone else had left the scene of the crime, and the list goes on and on. The ones I think of often now are the family members who suffer as a result of what many of these professionals have to live with and, in the case of those who manage the cases, the hours the professionals have to spend away from home in order to make things happen.

The Truth Will Set You Free

The ancient Greek philosopher Heraclitus wrote, "Justice will overtake fabricators of lies and false witnesses." Testifying in a murder trial was hard to get used to for the first little while, especially while the prosecutor was taking me through the events around the murder. It became suddenly easier as the defense lawyers began trying to rip apart my version of events. I was by no means smarter than these lawyers, but it seemed they were fighting a losing battle. The difficulty the lawyers were having was that they were trying to fight the truth with their clients' lies.

This is the second thing I learned during that trial, and it is something that has helped to change my life forever. The second thing I learned is that the best weapon on the stand is the truth. After the trial, I carried that lesson into my daily living, and it has given me a freedom I never thought possible. There are few battles we cannot win, on the stand or elsewhere, if we just speak truth.

Ten years after the last conviction of those I helped to put away, one of them received a new trial. The prosecutors wanted me to review material from the earlier trial. I wasn't interested. I did not even go back and read my own book describing in detail what had happened. I did not have to.

The truth of what happened that day is burned in my memory forever. Once again, the defendant was found guilty and sentenced to life in prison.

Life and Death

As I arrived back home after spending almost ten days on the stand, I stepped through my front door and threw my luggage into the closet. As I sat down at the kitchen table, Tina brought me a coffee and asked me how things had gone. That was an interesting question. How had things gone?

I stared off into our back yard, watching my rottweiler. He was one hundred and sixty pounds, trained, disciplined, and dangerous. I watched as he played in the yard like a harmless pup. In light of the question asked, the picture I was looking at seemed all the more intriguing. Neil had considered Wayne his rottweiler, and Wayne had passed on the same handle to Tina. The title was obviously intended to emphasize the dangerous nature of the individuals receiving the name and instill fear in those around them. It was that same instilled fear that had contributed to my heart attack only weeks before I was to face Neil and his rottweilers in court.

As I watched the dog frolic without a care in the world, I thought back to when I was young and Wayne was in university and on his way to playing pro football. I remembered that back then he would take kids from the hood and teach them sports rather than the ways of the streets. I remembered how he had bought diapers for my daughter fourteen years earlier and how much fun we had had on his wedding day. I remembered when Wayne the rottweiler had been Wayne the pup, who just enjoyed life and was determined to make a success of his life regardless of the obstacles.

They were thoughts like these that had brought tears to my eyes when I had been sitting on the stand staring into Wayne's eyes. I had looked past him then into the gallery, wondering if Mrs. James, his dear mother, was there or if she was now too frail to offer support. God knows she loved him and had tried to save him from himself.

How had things gone? I had almost forgotten the question while the memory of being on the stand rolled in my head. "They went well." I finally responded. "It was good to see Wayne again, and Neil is a goof." I did not mention Dino, so I assume I had no opinion on him whatsoever.

In the end, my fears turned mostly to sadness and hatred. All these years later, I have no real feelings left for any of them. We are all just dealing with the consequences of our own actions. They are serving life sentences, with the hope that maybe one day they will be free. As for me, that can be summed up in the answer I gave to one of the questions the lawyers put to me on the stand: "Is it true, Mr. Derry, that you were given immunity and therefore escaped a life sentence by testifying?" I responded by saying, "Yes, I traded it for a contract on my life." The lawyer had no further questions.

Lessons for Handlers

I have described two valuable lessons that I learned through the surreal experience of testifying at a major murder trial. I believe that if those who handle informants could learn these same two lessons and apply them, it would benefit them tremendously, especially when they are cultivating informants like me.

The first lesson would have been helpful for a handler that I had back in the 1980s just before Mike Cabana. This handler was from a municipal police force, and he was the only officer I can remember being deceitful with me on a constant basis. The lies were often petty or trivial, but all were detrimental from a relationship perspective. He lied to me about money on almost every deal that we had, and I could never trust him to be at a location on time. Both of these made it hard for me to put my life in his hands.

Deputy Commissioner Mike Cabana

Just as it is important on the witness stand, the truth is a key factor in the relationship between handlers and informants. In my mind, it does not seem beneficial for a handler to lie to the person who is living a lie for the handler. If the source is out betraying others and risking his life to find the truth in a dangerous world, it is crucial that there is someone that the informant can believe and trust in. In a world full of swirling waters of deceit, an informant needs a rock of truth to hold on to.

Another thing I have come to realize over the years is how much of a game the criminal and informant life used to be to me. In writing this chapter, I have been reminded again of the many people's lives that were affected by this one crime, the murder I have been talking about. But that also led me to realize how many people must have been affected by all the other crimes I was involved with ever since I entered the criminal world in the 1980s. Whatever was going on in my mind, it was not a game for the innocent victims and the innocent bystanders who were hurt by all those crimes.

I am not suggesting that all of the handlers and police officers around me considered their dealings with the criminal world to be a game as I did—but there were a few. Whether it was a coping mechanism, a lack of maturity, or some other reasons, I don't know. What I do know is that criminal investigation is not a competition in which the only outcome is adding another stroke to a scoreboard every time an arrest is made. The one thing informants like me could be taught by our handlers is the seriousness of what we are doing and the fact that our actions are going to have far-reaching effects on many, many people. I think at the same time it would not hurt handlers to learn the same lesson when cultivating people like me to use as informants.

I realize there are many protocols in place that touch on these issues. However, when officers are involved in the manipulation of lives, there needs to be more than a cursory, one-time glance at these lessons.

Life as a Rat

21

You learned the two greatest things in life: never rat on your friends, and always keep your mouth shut.

—Robert De Niro

There is not a day that goes by without a reminder that I spent my life betraying those I lived, worked, played, and ate with. If there is such a thing as a Judas complex, I am sure I invented it. If there is a specific thing that I can count on to remind me of my days as a rat, it is my ability to turn on and off the feelings I have for others. I don't know where it came from or how old I was when it started. I do know, however, that without that on–off switch, I would have committed suicide many years ago.

Take Care of My Boy

I had only been in the hood for about ten or fifteen minutes and had finished exchanging the customary handshakes with both true gangsters and wannabe gangsters. It seemed so out of place for a white guy to be receiving such a warm welcome in a predominantly black neighborhood every time I made an appearance. But I sucked up all that praise and attention just the same. In my head, I thought they were all nuts. I was there on behalf of the Hells Angels, filling their neighborhood with drugs. Why were they grateful? I thought Wayne James, my partner, was even more out of his mind. Why? It was not because he was an enforcer or because he was a hit man who would kill at a moment's notice. It was because he and the others in that black neighborhood seemed oblivious to the picture I was seeing. The Hells Angels were a white supremacist group, who despised the people they were doing business with.

I sucked up the praise and tried to ignore the odd glare that came from those who belonged to the working class in the area. The majority of these residents hated the crime in their community. If they had had their wish, the police would have taken all of us off to prison.

I then walked through the front door of the row house where Wayne was required to stay while he was out on parole. The first person I saw was his beautiful mother coming down the hall from her bedroom, still in her nightdress and pushing her walker. It was obvious from the look on her face that she had just gone to get her medication. Mrs. James had been suffering from bone cancer for a long time but never let it slow her down. I got a big hug from her and then a big hug from Wayne right after. It was a typical morning greeting. Wayne asked how the night had gone and if there were any problems he had to deal with that had arisen during our time apart.

Then Wayne's mother took me aside as if I had forgotten the words she spoke to me daily. It was as if she was the only one who got it in that whole damn neighborhood. I listened as if it was her first time telling me, "Paul, you take care of my boy. Keep him out of trouble, and don't let those phonies kill him." As usual, I hugged her and said, "That's why I am here, Mrs. James. I won't let anything happen." This frail, little lady who was about to cook me breakfast, this awesome woman who could barely walk or see, seemed to be the only one around who knew Wayne was flirting with death by being a pawn for a group who hated his race.

The words Mrs. James spoke to me over and over were screaming in my head the last time I saw Wayne before we met for a final time in a courtroom. It was at the apartment that the police had set up for me so that I could carry out a final operation. The phones and rooms were all wired, and everything was recorded. Wayne had called me on my cell phone, which was also being recorded, to tell me he was swinging by to grab some cash so he could get some beer for the game that night. I quickly went to the safe house, where I was fitted with a recording device, and then came back to the house to wait for Wayne to show.

It was a quick meeting but a memorable one for me. I am guessing it probably stands out in Wayne's mind now as well. I was engaged in the conversation, yet it seemed as if I was a million miles away. It is my guess that I was starting to distance myself mentally because of how difficult this last task with my friend was becoming. After a brief conversation, in which I tried to get one last admission recorded, it was done. I gave him a hug, told him I loved him, and headed back inside the apartment to wait for the dreaded but expected call.

Thirty minutes later, the calls from the hood started coming in. The police had just arrested Wayne under the guise of a parole violation. It would be another three weeks or so before he would finally realize that he was looking at a life sentence—and I was the rat who had set him up.

Catharine MacKinnon said, "It's particularly hard to take being stabbed in the back close to home. There's always a feeling of betrayal when people of your own group oppose you." I never saw or heard from Mrs. James again after that day, but I have heard her voice in my head every day for fourteen years now.

Cling Like a Barnacle

I would like to say that I was always able to use that inbred on–off switch to turn everything off, but that would be a lie. The one thing it could never help me with was the loneliness of being the betrayer. It was never easy to live between two worlds and be accepted by neither—and, in fact, usually be despised by both. The fear of a bullet to the head has never bothered me nearly as much as dealing with that empty space of time between the last takedown and the next job.

Sometimes, an informant is lucky enough to catch a break and find someone who takes his mind away from that empty world, even if that person is likely to end up being a target sometime in the future. I was lucky at least once.

Steve Gareau and I became friends shortly after I took over a failing drug business. I was in the process of climbing to the top of the ladder in hopes of getting close to the head of a criminal organization.

After serving a ten-year sentence for manslaughter for killing his best friend with an ax, Steve settled into the same small town where I was living. He had hopes and dreams of starting life over. Unfortunately, his family had passed away, most of his friends were now gone or would not talk to him, and he was carrying a cocaine addiction. Could it get much worse? I would like to say it couldn't, but the truth is that his life was about to spiral out of control and crash into a brick wall. Why was this? The answer is that informants like me are wonderful at turning people who can be useful to us into barnacles. And, in some cases, we become barnacles ourselves.

What does that look like? In Steve's case, his need for cocaine caused him to attach himself to whoever supplied his fix. In my case, I attached myself to others in order to go along for the ride and benefit from their labor. A good example is how I attached myself to Wayne for years and was able to use his violent reputation for my own benefit. The barnacle comparison is a good picture of the life of a rat—latching on to others and having others latch on to you. Then you just hang on for the ride while you pick up information along the way.

So, I become Steve's coke dealer, and I watched as he moved closer to me with each buy. I watched as he worked his way into becoming a great friend to my family. Then I started to use him, day after day. I would keep him in dope, and he would obey without hesitation every command I gave him. Steve was one of the smarter junkies, who knew not to bite the hand that fed him, and for this reason I could trust him to some extent. I say "to some extent" because I always had to put some restrictions on him if I sent him on an errand. It wasn't that he would steal my money or drugs on a delivery, but if I was not clear on when he had to be back, I might not see him for a couple of days.

I had taken Steve on a few trips to Canada's east coast over the spring and summer of 2000, and Steve fell in love with the place. The entire drive home on both trips was consumed with talk of him one day moving there and building a home. At the end of the second trip, I broke the news to Steve that I was moving back there. I told him what he already knew, that during that visit I had made a couple of connections that I thought would be worth the move. I told him he could come if he liked and I would pay his way. As ecstatic as he was, accepting my offer was truly the biggest mistake he ever made.

The trip to the east coast was hilarious, with Steve driving a jam-packed U-Haul truck behind me and my family in our little Toyota Cressida. We laughed at seeing his big grin behind us as he drove toward his dreamland, and we laughed with him on our breaks as he told us of his plans when he got there. It was during this trip that Steve really began to grow on me. I was starting to see him a little differently as we became closer.

When we arrived on the east coast, I took Steve aside and talked to him about the crime world in that area and a little about his drug addiction. I told him if he kept his drug use under control, I would start introducing him as my partner. That was a big deal for him; it would increase his income and build up his reputation. I made it very clear that the drugs could not get in the way and that if they did, he would be on his own.

I spent my time on the east coast around some heavy hitters, and before long I was reaching out for an operation. The crowd I traveled with were speaking about importing large quantities of drugs, they were talking a lot about developing local networks for drug distribution, and—most intriguing—they were discussing murder. It was a hard life for Steve to get used to, but the ten years he had spent in prison helped him to survive and to be accepted.

I remember getting a call from Wayne one time in the middle of the night. He asked me to get over to the hood as quickly as I could and to bring guns. Tina and I went in one car, and Steve went in another. Each of us had a gun, and Tina carried one for Wayne. When we pulled up, we had no idea what we were getting into, so we were cautious. Tina and I pulled into the parking lot first, while Steve pulled in behind us, blocking the entrance with his car. The three of us then spread out and walked toward a gathering of men yelling and screaming. When we spotted Wayne, Steve stayed back a little, while Tina and I walked up on either side of him. Wayne was yelling at Vincent Ross, a big, tough guy who reminded me of Mike Tyson. Vince was in a second floor window yelling at Wayne to fight him without weapons. Tina slid the .32 into Wayne's hand, and Wayne fired three shots off at Vince. That he did not hit him is amazing. We later found two of the bullet holes in the kitchen wall right behind where Vince had been standing. He had to have felt the breeze as the bullets flew past.

Steve was cool and held his own throughout the entire ordeal, but when it was over, he was asking for a fix. The deeper I got in with the gangsters, the deeper Steve sank into drug use, and the less he became useful to me. In the following months, we had both sunk to our lowest level. I was so addicted to the idea of pulling off a great operation, and he was so addicted to the idea of getting a great hit that neither of us could see what was coming. Three gunshots jarred us back into reality as Sean Simmons's body crumpled to the ground. We had both gotten so caught up in pursuing our own agendas that we were taken off guard when we ended up in the middle of a murder.

It was time for my departure from the criminal life, time for me to turn off my switch permanently and enter that space in time between operations. This operation had obviously gone sideways, and I almost had not made it out alive. It seemed that many things had not worked out as they should have. I wish Steve could have had the chance to start over—much sooner than the end of the twenty-five-year sentence he is currently serving. I liked Steve, I enjoyed his company, I wish him well, but unfortunately, like most people around me, he eventually ended up as a target.

It's an Addiction

Being a rat probably does not sound like a very appealing way of life. In fact, for most people, I am guessing it is quite the opposite. To make friends and then betray them is not pretty. Nor is it fun. However, every now and then my work would lead to a good arrest, which would make it all worthwhile. But each time I got that good arrest, it just fed the addiction to get more. I have contributed to many great takedowns throughout my career. They were enough to sustain me through all the bad aspects of that life, but never enough to quench the drive to keep doing it—not even now, when there is a bullet out there waiting to find me as its target.

Witness Protection and Starting Over

22

Everything has to come to an end, sometime.

—L. Frank Baum
The Marvelous Land of Oz

The number 187—which is usually spoken as "one eight seven" by police officers—refers to the crime of murder, the unlawful taking of life. In the case of a well-known Hells Angels associate turned police informant, Aimee Simard, it is the number of stab wounds in his body when he was found dead in his prison cell.

There are not many retirement options for a person who has spent his life as a police informant. Aimee was able to experience two of those options: he was first sentenced to life in prison, and then he was executed while serving that sentence.

Aimee's partner in crime was a member of the Hells Angels who was also a police informant. He thought he had finally made the big score, gotten his hands on the million-dollar payoff that every die-hard informant dreams about. Danny Kane negotiated a deal with the police that would make him one of the highest paid rats in Canadian history. Unfortunately for Danny, his life would soon be snuffed out. His death was not quite the same as the death of his partner and gay lover Aimee. Danny's demise came in a garage in a suburb of Montreal and is surrounded in mystery—Danny was said to have taken his own life.

I could name dozens of informants who have ended their careers by losing their lives or their freedom. However, these two examples are sufficient to show the true picture—being an informant is not a risk-free kind of job. It is only the lucky few who end up in one of the many witness protection programs that are available. I consider myself just that, one of the lucky ones. I have had the privilege of cheating death many times, and after cheating both death and a life sentence, I was fortunate enough to be able to enter Canada's federal witness protection program.

Disorientation

It is nearly impossible to encapsulate in words what takes place when someone is taken from an absolutely antisocial world, stripped of his identity, cleaned up, and then suddenly inserted into a totally prosocial environment as a regular joe. There is some serious culture shock to say the least. To say it comes with a sense of disorientation would be a huge understatement. Relating some of my experiences will give a sense of what it is like.

Actress Sheridan Smith said, "When you're hiding behind a character all the time, as soon as you have to be yourself, you feel kind of terrified." It is probably pretty accurate to say that I was "kind of terrified" when I entered the witness protection program. But what I was terrified of is probably not what most people would have guessed. Most people assume that I was scared of the Hells Angels. There is some truth to that to be sure. I certainly did not want to be kidnapped and put through whatever torture they might decide to inflict on me once they had me alone and isolated. However, the truth of the matter is that fear of the Hells Angels was fairly low on my list of fears. My biggest fear was of society itself. I was scared of starting over in a system that I did not begin to understand. I was certainly adept at mimicking or copying the ways of prosocial living, but I really had no idea of the mechanics of what made it tick.

There is something quite liberating about starting completely over as a new person. Placed in a new location, with a new name and no history to follow, I could be anyone I wanted to be. However, at the same time, there were a lot of little things that popped up each day that nearly drove me crazy. There were many things that bothered me that I could never have imagined when I signed my old life away. There were things that I had left behind that caused me unimaginable emotional turmoil, and there were habits that were ingrained from my old life that would pop up unexpectedly. Let me give some examples:

1. *Things that made me crazy.* In the first year, I am guessing that I signed "Paul Derry" or put down my old social security number at least fifty times. When doing simple things like getting electricity hooked up at my place or getting a phone under my new name, I would automatically start to fill in my old information. I ripped up more applications for different things—followed by having to explain that I had made a mistake—than I ever care to remember.

2. *Things that bothered me.* This may not bother female informants as much as males, but giving up my surname was a huge ordeal for me. As men, we tend to grow up with an expectation that we will carry on the family name. It still bothers me to this day that I had to stop using my dad's name and that it will not carry on to the next generation.

3. *Things left behind, causing emotional turmoil.* It naturally seems like a good thing to leave behind the things that will hurt you or the bad things that you once carried around with you. The unfortunate

thing is that, like my surname, I had to give up a lot of good things along with the bad. It brought a sickening feeling to walk away from my ancestry and my history in general. But it is hard to explain what it was like to walk away from my parents, siblings, children, and friends, knowing that they were still alive but that I would likely never see them again.

All of these things take their toll. The last two categories especially can cause serious emotional turmoil if you do not learn quickly how to deal with them. However, it was the ingrained habits that seemed to be the hardest for me to overcome.

Old Habits

Kenneth Schwarz has said, "If breaking a habit has been hard for you to do, hard for you even to face, then a helping hand is in order."

If starting life over with a new identity was liberating, it was old habits and my old nature that threatened to imprison me all over again and send me back to the life I had once lived. I suppose that would be true in general for anyone trying to make a fresh start in life, but for someone going from an antisocial life in which every one of the Ten Commandments was broken in extreme ways, it was even more difficult. In fact, there were some days that, no matter how much I wanted to change, I wondered if my mind would ever be renewed.

When I first arrived at my new location under the witness protection program, I joined a local church. I thought that if I was going to avoid making friends with people from the circles I had once traveled in, then a church would be my best bet. After all, it seemed unlikely that the Hells Angels would frequent a place populated by those attempting to avoid hell. At the very least, a church seemed a better option than bars and strip joints. The first church I joined was a small nondenominational group who seemed quite tightly knit. This group offered a lot of the things that the criminal community had once provided for me: a sense of community, nonjudgmental acceptance, and a feeling of brotherhood. In short, it was a place where I felt I belonged. The difference was that there was a peace and a commitment to one another in the church that I had never experienced in organized crime.

One day, a couple of outsiders showed up at the front door of the church shortly after the worship service. It seemed they had some problem with the pastor that he was very quietly trying to resolve with them. I was keeping an eye on the three of them as I talked to one of the other members of the church. Suddenly, the tone of the other conversation started to sound much more confrontational. As the situation seemed to be getting out of hand, I went over and told the outsiders to chill out or they were going to be dealing with me rather than the pastor. They were both fairly big guys, and when they cursed back at me, asking what I thought I was going to do, I lost it and told them they would soon find out. I quickly went to the back of the church, where I knew there was a toolbox. It was my intention to grab an equalizer and show these two exactly what I was capable of doing about it.

When I reached the back room to grab some sort of weapon to prove my point, my good friend was back there, and he asked me what it was I was looking for. I explained the situation and told him I was looking for something to hit them with. His response was simple, but it stopped me in my tracks, making me think about what I was contemplating. I realized how quickly my mind had reverted to its old habits of thought. My friend said, "Try hitting them with this," as he held up his Bible.

This would not be the last time or the only setting in which I was inclined to resort to my habitual use of violence to deal with an issue. My ways slowly changed, but it was an ongoing struggle.

Finances and Bookkeeping

Another big area where I faced a real challenge was the area of finances and business. One of my first business ventures in my new world was a small restaurant. It was actually more of a coffee shop, but it had a kitchen and was strategically located in a government building. If there was anything that facilitated my journey into prosocial living, it was this venture, even though at the time it felt like a crazy nightmare. The first thing I thought when I started this business was: "How the hell does anyone live on the money made in something like this?" After all, I was used to spending tens of thousands of dollars a week on myself, and now I was trying to make a living by earning forty cents on a cup of coffee while serving people who complained constantly. Unfortunately, it took a long time and the loss of a lot of prized possessions before I learned that my old spending habits had to change.

If the finances were hard to learn, the bookkeeping nearly drove me out of my mind. The best way to contrast it to my old world is to describe a typical meeting with bikers years earlier.

It was 1996, and I was on my way to see a high-ranking member of a Hells Angels puppet club called The Undertakers. It was a meeting in which I was going to drop off money for a pound of cocaine that I had borrowed while waiting for my connection to reload. When I walked into the house, we headed to the basement, where I handed over the cash without saying a word. The member then took out a pen and paper, and we carried on our business by writing each question and answer on a piece of paper, all the while talking about superficial topics such as the weather and our plans for the day. When we were finished with our business, including discussing the product I needed, prices, quality, and comparisons to what the competition was offering, we took the sheet of paper and burned it, leaving the ashes in an ashtray.

No wonder I was struggling with the concept of bookkeeping in my new world. After living for years in a world where I had done everything possible to keep no records of my business transactions, I now had to learn to make a record of every transaction and account for every penny. I can tell you that transition did not come easy.

Debt collecting and dealing with delinquent accounts was a strange thing to get used to also. This became even more difficult when I bought rental properties and had to deal with people not paying their rent. Being a landlord certainly had some things in common with being a coke dealer, including tracking down those who were trying to evade paying at the end of every month. I was already familiar with sitting at the end of driveways hoping to catch the evaders before they spent my money on something else. Now, most tenants paid on time and without incident, but there were always a few I had to chase down, just as I had chased down those who had tried to skip out on paying their drug bills. So why was tracking down those who owed me rent so hard to get used to? In the real world, I could not use physical force. Instead, I had to follow rules and procedures, something I had formerly found very difficult to manage.

Being Hunted

Bomber suspect Richard Jewell recalled, "I felt like a hunted animal, followed constantly, waiting to be killed."

I said at the beginning of this chapter that some of these other things were more terrifying than the knowledge that the Hells Angels wanted to kill me. But make no mistake about it. I am in no way trying to downplay the reality of being hunted. I am now closer to the end of my life than the beginning, and I have much less fear than I probably should have. That, coupled with the fact that I do not believe that the majority in society should ever give in to the intimidation of the few, makes it even more difficult to walk in trepidation. However, I do walk in caution, and I do take into consideration that members of my family have most of their lives ahead of them. This leads to issues that, if I was alone, would probably not have affected my life as much as they have while I have been hunted over the past fourteen years.

One of the biggest effects of my being hunted during these past few years is how often we have had to move. The fact that I and my family have been forced to live a very nomadic lifestyle has been a blessing and a curse. The blessing has been that geography is one of the easiest things to teach my children. The curse is that we have never been able to settle and call any place home.

Better Option

There may be another ending to the life of an informant besides the ones I have mentioned. If there is, I do not know what it is, nor have I seen any examples of it. This is particularly true for those who have chosen the life of an informant as a long-term venture. Here, I will say something similar to what I have said in earlier chapters: if the police are going to cultivate informants, especially on a long-term basis, then it is imperative that they have a plan. It is imperative that they help the informant plan for the future and that they facilitate an eventual exit strategy for the informant. Recruitment will be more difficult as long as the primary retirement options are death and imprisonment.

Final Thoughts

23

Knowing others is intelligence; knowing yourself is true wisdom. Mastering others is strength; mastering yourself is true power.

—Tao Te Ching

The idea to write this book first arose after many police officers suggested I should speak at source handling courses. Although the thought seemed intriguing, I had never done any public speaking and really did not believe I had much to offer trained officers in addition to what they had already been taught. However, after many more nights of sitting in hotel rooms and safe houses with police officers from a wide variety of departments and jurisdictions, I started seeing a common thread: they all seemed interested in picking my brain regarding my work as an informant. The revelation that I had a head full of information that seemed valuable in police officers' eyes was reinforced by the fact that many officers were passing my first book around, encouraging others to read it. Together, these two factors convinced me that I should consider sharing what I had experienced.

I started to research books that had been written on the subject of being a police informant and found two things. First, the books that had been published were mainly written by former police officers or criminologists. Second, the few books that I could find that had been written by informants tended to be focused on the informants' exploits and bragging about their successes rather than being honest accounts of how informants manipulate the system.

Robert F. Kennedy stated, "The purpose of life is to contribute in some way to making things better." It became my mission to write a book that would make at least a small difference for good in the world. Therefore, I determined to write an interesting book that would hold readers' attention by relating some stories about the dangerous work that informants do. I also determined to write a useful book by pointing out some perils and pitfalls that are common in police officers' handling of informants. It is my hope that this book has met both of these objectives.

Across North America and around the world, police officers are recruiting informants every day. Some do this with an understanding of their duty and the care that is owed to the informant as a human being, while others seem to lack that understanding.

In the final chapter of this book, I would like to focus attention on some serious flaws in the way police officers have cultivated informants, including some who should never have been chosen for the job; revisit some wise words from a pair of great cops whom I now consider to be friends rather than handlers; and, finally, offer some suggestions for improvements in the handling of informants.

Reckless

Luke Shuman observed, "In exchange for leniency, untrained informants are sent out to perform dangerous police operations with few legal protections." This observation sums up one of the most significant issues when it comes to the cultivation of informants, especially in the United States, where many questionable methods have been used in the war on drugs.

LeBron Gaither was a sixteen-year-old student in Lebanon, Kentucky. One afternoon, Gaither experienced an outburst of anger in which he punched the school's assistant principal in the jaw. He was taken into custody as a juvenile and charged with assault. An officer approached him while he was in custody and told him that he could either face a jail sentence or become a confidential informant. Gaither signed the paperwork and soon began performing undercover drug operations. By the time he turned eighteen, Gaither had participated in many of these operations.

Shortly after his eighteenth birthday, Gaither was called before a grand jury in a closed session to testify against Jason Noel, a local drug dealer and his latest target. The very next day, the police sent Gaither out again with a wire and cash to buy more drugs from Noel. It was a decision that a former state's attorney called the most "reckless, stupid and idiotic idea" he had seen in his nearly twenty years as a prosecutor.

The meeting took place in the parking lot of a local grocery store. Gaither had been told by police not to get into the target's car. Once he had the drugs in hand, he had been instructed to say, "This looks good," and at that point the police would move in for the arrest. If something went wrong, Gaither had been instructed to say, "I wish my brother was here." This would signal officers to quickly move in and arrest Noel.

Unfortunately, a member of the grand jury had informed Noel that Gaither was a rat. Shortly after the meeting began, the detectives lost track of Gaither when Noel convinced Gaither to get into his car and drove off with him.

Gaither was eventually found. He had been tortured, beaten with a bat, shot with both a pistol and a shotgun, run over by a car, and dragged by a chain through the woods.

Dangerous

Jeremy Mitchell was an avid weight lifter and worked hard at the construction job that his father had helped him to get. Mitchell loved both lifting weights and hard labor jobs, but, after hurting his back, he struggled with both activities and started taking pain pills. Unfortunately, he did not have a prescription for the pills that were most effective at taking away the constant pain he was in, and he had to get them elsewhere. One day in 2006, after acquiring medication for himself, he agreed to sell eight methadone pills to a friend. It turned out that the friend was wearing a wire, and Mitchell was now facing a potential jail sentence. According to his father, a narcotics agent gave Jeremy two options: make a deal or go to prison. Jeremy signed a contract and became a confidential informant.

Mitchell had set up at least five drug suspects. However, he was told that that was not enough because the cases had led to plea bargains rather than to convictions. Mitchell felt trapped and kept on working until he had more than a dozen operations under his belt. This placed him in a very dangerous predicament, and he was becoming more nervous with each takedown.

Mitchell's fourteenth operation led to the arrest of William Vance Reagan, Jr., a heroin trafficker who was released on bail after only one day in jail. A week later, Reagan phoned Mitchell's mother, saying, "Tell your son I'm out of jail and that he better watch his back." Mitchell immediately told his police handler, his mother later said, but the officer seemed unconcerned, saying, "Don't worry about it—the guy's harmless."

On December 29, 2008, Mitchell left his house to buy some milk. He never returned. Instead, he was lured to a nearby home, where he was shot with a .22 caliber pistol three times in the back of the head and then once, at close range, in the face.

At his trial, Reagan bragged to the judge that he had done the world a favor by getting rid of another rat. One news account said he told the court, "Anybody that Jeremy knew or came into contact with would have been suffering for it" and "The good of the many outweighs the good of the few." Reagan was sentenced to a well-deserved life sentence with no possibility of parole.

But Jeremy Mitchell was still dead.

Rachel's Law

On May 7, 2009, a piece of legislation known as "Rachel's Law" was passed by the state of Florida. This new law required police agencies in Florida to rethink the cultivation and use of police informants, especially those who were being rewarded with lighter sentences for petty crimes. Rachel's Law requires law enforcement agencies to

1. Provide special training for officers who recruit confidential informants
2. Instruct informants that reduced sentences might not be provided in exchange for their work
3. Permit informants to request a lawyer if they want one

This law was certainly a good start toward changing the mentality of police officers, some of whom had been looking at informants as just tools and not human beings with lives, families, and friends. It was also a small step toward convincing police forces that informants are not indispensable.

What brought about this small but meaningful shift in thinking? It was the death of a young Florida woman who had been pressured into acting as an informant and who had lost her life as a result.

On May 7, 2008, twenty-three-year-old Rachel Hoffman got into her silver Volvo sedan with $13,000 in marked bills. At approximately 6:30 that evening, she texted her boyfriend, saying, "I just got wired up" and "Wish me luck, I'm on my way."

Hoffman seems to have been at ease, knowing that nineteen law enforcement agents were tracking her every move and that a drug enforcement surveillance plane was circling overhead. But Rachel Hoffman was by no means a trained narcotics operative.

A few weeks earlier, police officers had come to Hoffman's apartment after a neighbor had reported that she might be dealing marijuana. When asked if she had any illegal substances inside, Hoffman had said yes and had given the officers permission to come in and conduct a search. After police had found about five ounces of pot and a small quantity of pills, Hoffman had been informed that she could be facing a lengthy prison sentence. The officer in charge had then told her that she could help herself if she would act as a confidential informant.

Hoffman had decided this was her best way out, as she wanted to avoid going to prison. Although she had never given information as a source in any capacity, she was now on her way to conduct a major undercover operation. It was an operation in which she would be required to meet with two convicted felons alone in her car in order to buy cocaine, ecstasy pills, and a handgun.

The operation did not go as planned or anywhere close to it. Within an hour, the cover team had lost track of Hoffman.

Two days after Hoffman disappeared, her body was found in a ravine overgrown with tangled vines. Hoffman had been shot five times in the chest and head with the gun that the police had sent her to buy.

Rachel Hoffman was just one of the thousands of people who are enlisted each year to help the police bust others, often in exchange for a promise of leniency in the criminal justice system. Unfortunately, she was also not exceptional in that her undercover work led to her being killed.

The three examples I have given demonstrate the importance of regulations—and the enforcement of those regulations—when it comes to the cultivation and use of confidential informants and agents. After all, it is people's lives that are on the line, and certainly no one deserves to die just because he or she dabbled in marijuana or was guilty of some other minor crime at a relatively young age.

On the other hand, let's not be naïve. Many of those used as confidential informants are not petty criminals committing minor crimes. In fact, more often than not, confidential informants are people like me who are very well versed in the workings of both the criminal world and the justice system. As I have stated many times, the reality is that it takes a killer to catch a killer. Or, as Shane Halliday once said, "If all we ever use are altar boys, all we will ever catch are priests." Looking at drug cases alone, it is estimated that eighty-five percent of the cases brought to court have reached this stage with the help of informants. My own guess is that the percentage is closer to ninety-eight percent, but I may be biased.

The Handler's Perspective

In this book, I have used many quotes from Deputy Commissioner Mike Cabana of the RCMP and former homicide detective Shane Halliday. I did so for two reasons. First, they exemplify everything I believe a police officer should be. Second, and more important, they possess all the skills of a great handler. There have been many others whom I have met over the years who were similarly gifted. It takes a team, not an individual, to do a great job of policing. However, these two were by far the best examples in my dealings with police officers over the past thirty years.

I have already quoted extensively from the following thoughts expressed by Mike Cabana. However, I feel these thoughts are worth repeating as a whole, rather than just inserting a few isolated quotes from them at various points throughout this book. These thoughts arose out of a discussion we had regarding the character traits/skills needed to be a successful handler:

Flexibility/reliability: Anyone getting involved in this line of work needs to realize that information does not surface on a set schedule, Monday to Friday, 8:00 a.m. to 4:00 p.m. Furthermore, a handler needs to understand that the information being provided is seen as a source of revenue by the informant.

If the handler fails to follow through with the information, there is a financial impact to the informant. Too many missed opportunities will lead, in some cases, to the informant losing interest.

Innovative thinking: I quickly realized that the information being provided and/or the circumstances around the criminal activity the info related to seldom fit into a textbook case type of investigation. If something can go sideways, it inevitably will, and the handler needs to be prepared to figure out the best way forward.

Problem solving: Informants are people, and many of them bring significant baggage and regularly need assistance navigating through personal issues/events affecting them. A handler needs to be prepared to help to the extent possible. This is very much a two-way relationship.

Results-oriented/teamwork: I think a handler needs to remain focused on the end result while ensuring the activities of the informant do not cross the proverbial line. A good handler also needs to understand that he/she is part of a much broader team and needs to be able to engage the support of other members (and sometimes people outside the organization) while ensuring the security/safety of the informant. Safety of the informant needs to remain the primary focus, and a handler needs to be prepared to walk away from good information if he/she feels it may compromise the safety of the informant.

Some of the basic skills, though, have not changed over the years. I think a good handler needs fairly strong communication skills and some degree of intellectual dexterity. What do I mean by this? Building rapport and understanding individual motivators is extremely helpful to this work. A good handler possesses an ability to easily observe/listen to sources and analyze what they say/don't say/exhibit in body language and read their character strengths/weaknesses and motivators. With this information, he/she can use strategies to subtly persuade and influence the person. This is where the intellectual dexterity comes in. You need to read these cues, interpret them and start to use them all at the same time. The advanced skills in interpretation can be taught, but communication skills and the ability to 'think on your feet,' so to speak, have to be there.

A handler also needs a good knowledge of policy and case law and the common sense and integrity to use it properly with constant vigilance toward risk management. At the higher end, [there needs to be] knowledge of major investigative techniques, so you can understand how to get the information out in a timely fashion, in the proper form and in such a way that it protects your source. [There need to be] tactical awareness and a concern for safety at the higher end when handling high access or principal sources, [a concern] for the safety of the handlers and for the safety (duty of care) of the source.

To sum it up…it all comes back to communication and the ability to build rapport. In the absence of these, all these other skills are for naught because without these essential two skills, you will not be able to develop or handle sources. Some people can communicate and build rapport naturally, and others can learn. Some simply cannot.

Last Words

I would love to leave Mike with the last word, but that would be just a little out of character for me—and God knows I do not like to be out of character.

This book presents my perspective on the shadowy world that I spent years roaming through. It is a glimpse into my mind and how I look at that world of insanity. As you can tell, I have spent a great deal of time thinking about handlers and the job that they perform. I believe that if they can begin to see the importance of their role in an informant's life, it will benefit all who are affected by the work being done.

There are a few final thoughts that I would like to offer before bringing this book to a close. The first six chapters, which make up Section I of this book, discussed just how sneaky, manipulative, and dangerous an informant can be. They also discussed how dangerous the playground is in which criminals and informants choose to amuse themselves, a playground whose dangers should be obvious to any rational human being. The next eleven chapters discussed the characteristics that police officers should have and, even more importantly, the characteristics that police officers who handle informants must possess. Why is it vital for a handler to possess these qualities? It is simple. Without these qualities, the manipulative bastards described in Section I will control the handlers described in Section II, rather than the other way around.

> Some day...after I am dead, you may perhaps come to learn the right and wrong of this. I cannot tell you.
>
> **—Robert Louis Stevenson**
> *The Strange Case of Dr. Jekyll and Mr. Hyde*

Appendix A: Police Perspectives on Paul Derry as a Source

In view of Derry's capabilities to supply good information due to his close association to some of Moncton area's most prominent drug traffickers/criminals and the fact that his probation was a result of a minor criminal offence, consideration should be given for Derry to become a coded human source.

—**Mike Cabana**
March 28, 1988

Source (Derry) has worked as an agent for RCMP Moncton Drugs and was successful in introducing an undercover operator to numerous drug dealers.

—**Constable Dan Rowter**
Bridgewater RCMP, September 12, 1990

Throughout the operation, J-1028 (Derry) displayed a high level of dedication toward the objectives of the job and earned a certain level of credibility with the writer for being observant, truthful and dependable.

—**Bob Powers**
Moncton Drugs, September 13, 1990

Source (Derry) continues to provide valuable information/intelligence on the Hells Angels and their close associates. These sections, as well as others, are interested in pursuing this information further.

—**Constable G.H. Clarke**
July 15, 1996

Derry travels in the local drug sub-culture circles in the Brockville/Prescott areas. He would be an excellent tool to infiltrate the local drug traffickers.

—**Constable J.C. Rennick**
Kingston Drug Section, October 1, 1999

On this date, Halifax Regional Police Department will be concluding their investigation, which used the services of H-885 (Derry) in the agent capacity. They will be arresting three local persons for first degree murder and at the same time arresting a full patch member of the Hells Angels. This member is the person who ordered the murder of Sean Simmons to occur. The charging of the Hells member is significant and will have a tremendous impact on the overall criminal activity within the metro area.

—**Corporal Al Comeau**
April 17, 2001

Appendix B: Words between a Source and His Handlers

The following quotations, in addition to others that have been used throughout this book, help to illuminate the issues and character traits of handlers and informants. The ones from Mike Cabana are drawn from conversations throughout our years of working together.

> Some members of the public think that the police only catch bad guys and bother innocent citizens, but they do many things that the public would never think of and many would not want to deal with. With some of the things that I and other members have seen over the years, you sometimes wonder just how bad mankind can be to others as well as themselves. For many years, when members completed a call of a traumatic nature, they were expected to just suck it up and get on with their job. Now they have employee assistance programs where members can talk about and deal with events that they have dealt with. During my time on the job, I attended many calls that were of a traumatic nature, and many of these are buried in my memory; everything from baby deaths [to] homicides where victims were shot, stabbed or beaten to death, suicides and sudden deaths. Some of them were worse than others, depending on the nature of the injuries, the age of the victim, how long the remains had been there and the method of death. When you see what humans can do to themselves or others, it can affect you. A lot of old time cops just buried it, and it affected them in many ways, some having a morbid and dark sense of humor in order to deal with what they had seen and dealt with. There are things that I still remember as clearly as the day they happened and probably always will, and I just try not to think about them. It was all part of being a cop, the part that the public probably doesn't know about and many would say, 'They are just doing their job.'

> —Shane Halliday

On November 29/30 Sgt. HALLIDAY drafted and later swore to a warrant to Search a residence located at _____. The warrant was executed during the early morning hours of November 30th, and a quantity of stolen firearms were recovered and three subjects arrested. As a further result of interviews of the three subjects in custody, further information was received concerning threats against the president of the United States.

The president was scheduled to arrive in Halifax the next day. As a result of information received, Sgt. HALLIDAY prepared two other warrants to Search, resulting in three more people being arrested, two other stolen firearms [being] recovered, and charges being laid in regards to the threats against the president of the United States. Files _____ refer. Sgt. HALLIDAY worked over 36 hours straight during this period, which exemplifies his attentiveness and commitment to duty.

Because of these threats against the president, these files receive much attention from several different agencies, including the United States Secret Service, the agency responsible for protecting the president.

Excellent work by Sgt. HALLIDAY, which made the local police services look very good.

—Excerpt from a 2004 letter about Shane Halliday's work

I have never tried to influence your decisions, I have never lied to you, nor to my knowledge misdirected you; I do not intend to start today.

—Mike Cabana

All along I have done my best to show compassion, consideration and help as much as I could.

—Mike Cabana

I can't help but realize that in many ways it is likely that we would not be here if it were not for your hard work and patience over the years. It's about investing in lives…I choose to believe you invested in mine in the meaningful way that you did due to the integrity and compassion you walk in. If not, and you did it because it was a job, then rest assured the result was the same as if you had the right motive.

—Paul Derry

Trust me…I had the right motive and still do. That's what makes some decisions so hard.

—Mike Cabana

All I can do is hope that you know me well enough to know that when I set my mind on doing something, it usually happens. It may take time, I may piss off a few people in the process, but eventually it does happen.

—Mike Cabana

As I said in the past, it is important for you to be guided by your conscience and what you think is right.

—**Mike Cabana**

I have always been honest in my dealings with you and have always tried my best to help. That will never change.

—**Mike Cabana**

In identifying those key attributes/competencies, I think it's important to first identify what a successful handler will deliver, as I believe there are different definitions that can be considered. From a purely organizational perspective, success can be defined as the ability to control and extract information from individuals in support of ongoing investigations or to prevent the commission of offences. Another definition (which I believe to be more appropriate) would be the ability to fairly work with individuals having close contact with criminals to secure information to prevent crime [and] assist ongoing investigations, while protecting the integrity and safety of the individual. There is a significant difference between the two.

—**Mike Cabana**

If it's all the same to you, I would rather not have to deal with disgruntled Paul again.

—**Mike Cabana**

Index